INFORMATION RISK
MANAGEME

CW00925267

BCS, THE CHARTERED INSTITUTE FOR IT

BCS, The Chartered Institute for IT champions the global IT profession and the interests of individuals engaged in that profession for the benefit of all. We promote wider social and economic progress through the advancement of information technology science and practice. We bring together industry, academics, practitioners and government to share knowledge, promote new thinking, inform the design of new curricula, shape public policy and inform the public.

Our vision is to be a world-class organisation for IT. Our 70,000 strong membership includes practitioners, businesses, academics and students in the UK and internationally. We deliver a range of professional development tools for practitioners and employees. A leading IT qualification body, we offer a range of widely recognised qualifications.

Further Information
BCS, The Chartered Institute for IT,
First Floor, Block D,
North Star House, North Star Avenue,
Swindon, SN2 1FA, United Kingdom.
T +44 (0) 1793 417 424 ·
F +44 (0) 1793 417 444
www.bcs.org/contact

http://shop.bcs.org/

INFORMATION RISK MANAGEMENT

A practitioner's guide

David Sutton

First South Asian Edition 2016

Permission to reproduce extracts from British Standards is granted by BSI. British Standards can be obtained in PDF or hard copy formats from the BSI online shop: www.bsigroup.com/Shop or by contacting BSI Customer Services for hardcopies only: Tel: +44 (0)20 8996 9001, Email: cservices@bsigroup.com.

Published by BCS Learning & Development Ltd, a wholly owned subsidiary of BCS The Chartered Institute for IT, First Floor, Block D, North Star House, North Star Avenue, Swindon, SN2 1FA, UK. www.bcs.org

ISBN: 978-1-78017-265-1

This edition is for sale in Indian subcontinent only. Not for export elsewhere.

British Cataloguing in Publication Data.
A CIP catalogue record for this book is available at the British Library.

BCS books are available at special quantity discounts to use as premiums and sale promotions, or for use in corporate training programs. Please visit our Contact us page at www.bcs.org/contact

Typeset by Lapiz Digital Services, Chennai, India.
Printed and bound in India
Digitally Printed at Replika Press Pvt. Ltd

It is through the gradual development of trust and respect that acquaintances and colleagues become friends.

From 2001 to 2010 I had the great privilege of working with a group of highly dedicated people from the UK Cabinet Office, the Department for Business, Innovation and Skills, Ofcom, and organisations representing the whole of the electronic communications industry. Many of us still meet socially at The Old Shades in Whitehall from time to time.

This book is for Fred Micklewright, whose insight, support and wisdom made the work a pleasure.

CONTENTS

LIST OF FIGURES AND TABLES

AUTHOR

David Sutton's career spans more than 45 years and includes radio transmission, international telephone switching, computing, voice and data networking, structured cabling systems, information security and critical information infrastructure protection.

He joined Cellnet (now Telefónica UK) in 1993, where he was responsible for ensuring the continuity and restoration of the core cellular and broadband networks, and represented the company in the electronic communications industry's national resilience forum, the EC-RRG. In December 2005 he gave evidence to the Greater London Authority enquiry into the mobile telecoms impact of the London bombings.

David has been a member of the BCS Professional Certification Information Security Panel since 2005 and delivers lectures on information risk management and business continuity at the Royal Holloway, University of London, from which he holds an MSc in Information Security, and at which he is an external tutor on their open learning MSc course.

Since retiring from Telefónica UK in 2010, he has undertaken a number of critical information infrastructure projects for the European Network and Information Security Agency (ENISA), developed business continuity and information risk management training material for InfoSec Skills, and serves on the training accreditation panel for the Institute of Information Security Professionals (IISP).

David is a co-author of *Information Security Management Principles*, also published by BCS, ISBN 978-1-78017-175-3, now in its second edition.

ACKNOWLEDGMENTS

I would like to thank Jutta Mackwell and Matthew Flynn of BCS for kindly agreeing to publish this book; Karen Greening and Mary Hobbins for their invaluable guidance and for finding all my mistakes; and my wife Sharon for putting up with my more grumpy moments and for her unceasing encouragement.

ABBREVIATIONS

AIRMIC	Association of Insurance and Risk Managers
AS/NZS	Australian Standard/New Zealand Standard
BC	business continuity
BCI	Business Continuity Institute
BCM	business continuity management
BCS	BCS, The Chartered Institute for IT
BIA	business impact analysis
BIS	The Department for Business, Innovation and Skills
BPSS	baseline personnel security standard
BR	business resumption
BS	British Standard
BSI	British Standards Institute
BYOD	bring your own device
CCA	Civil Contingencies Act, 2004
CCP	CESG Certified Professional
CCTA	Central Computer and Telecommuncations Agency
CCTV	closed-circuit television
CD	compact disc
CDPA	Copyright, Designs and Patents Act, 1988
CESG	Communications-Electronics Security Group
CIA	confidentiality, integrity and availability
CIO	Chief Information Officer
CISO	Chief Information Security Officer
CLAS	CESG Listed Advisor Scheme
CMA	Computer Misuse Act, 1990
CMM	Capability Maturity Model
CNSS	Committee on National Security Systems
COMAH	control of major accident hazards
COMSO	Communications Security Officer
CPNI	Centre for the Protection of National Infrastructure
CRAMM	CCTA Risk Analysis and Management Method
CTC	counter-terrorist check
DAS	direct attached storage
DNA	Deoxyribonucleic acid

DMZ	demilitarised zone
DoS	denial of service
DDoS	distributed denial of service
DPA	Data Protection Act, 1998
DR	disaster recovery
DV	developed vetting
DVD	digital versatile disc
ENISA	European Network and Information Security Agency
EU	European Union
FAIR	factor analysis of information risk
FERMA	Federation of European Risk Management Associates
FoIA	Freedom of Information Act, 2000
GCHQ	Government Communications Head Quarters (UK)
GPG	good practice guide(lines)
GSI	Government Secure Intranet
HMG	Her Majesty's Government
IA	information assurance
IASME	information assurance for small and medium enterprises
ICT	information communications and technology
IEC	International Electro-technical Commission
IISP	Institute of Information Security Professionals
IM	incident management
IP	intellectual property
IP	Internet Protocol
IRAM	Information Risk Analysis Method
IRBC	ICT readiness for business continuity
IRM	Institute of Risk Management
ISF	Information Security Forum
ISMS	Information Security Management System
ISO	International Organisation for Standardisation
ISP	Internet service provider
IT	information technology
ITSO	IT Security Officer
ITU	International Telecommunication Union
LAN	local area network
MAO	maximum acceptable outage
MBCO	minimum business continuity objective
MR	mandatory requirement
MTDL	maximum tolerable data loss
MTPD	maximum tolerable period of disruption

NAS	network attached storage
NDA	non-disclosure agreement
NIST	National Institute for Standards and Technology
NSA	National Security Agency
NSV	national security vetting
OCTAVE	Operationally Critical Threat, Asset and Vulnerability Evaluation
OSA	Official Secrets Act, 1989
PAS	publicly available specification
PDA	personal digital assistant
PDCA	plan–do–check–act
PIN	personal identification number
PKI	Public Key Infrastructure
PP	Professional Practice (BCI)
PSN	Public Services Network
RAID	redundant array of inexpensive disks
RIPA	Regulation of Investigatory Powers Act, 2000
RMADS	Risk Management and Accreditation Document Set
RMR	risk management requirement
RPO	recovery point objective
RTO	recovery time objective
SABSA	Sherwood Applied Business Security Architecture
SAN	Storage area networks
SANS	Sysadmin, Audit, Network, Security
SC	security check
SFIA	Skills Framework for the Information Age
SIRA	Security and Information Risk Advisor
SIRO	Senior Information Risk Officer
SMB	server message block
SME	small and medium sized enterprises
SQL	Structured Query Language
SSID	service set identifier
TLP	Traffic Light Protocol
UPS	uninterruptible power supply
URL	uniform resource locator
VLAN	virtual local area network
VOIP	Voice Over Internet Protocol
VPN	virtual private network
Wi-Fi	Wireless Fidelity

DEFINITIONS, STANDARDS AND GLOSSARY OF TERMS

It is very helpful in any context, but especially in information risk management that we have a common understanding of the terminology used. For example, people often refer to risk when they actually mean threat without perhaps realising that there is a distinct difference.

In this section, we shall provide definitions of all the key terms used in information risk management, most of which originate in ISO Guide 73:2009 *Risk Management – Vocabulary*.

We shall then move on to cover the main national and international standards and good practice guidelines used in the management of information risk, and also identify where the reader can obtain them.

Risk management can be significantly more effective with clear and concise definitions:

> You can't effectively and consistently manage what you can't measure, and you can't measure what you haven't defined. (The Open Group Standard, Risk Taxonomy (O-RT), Version 2.0, October 2013)

Let us begin though, by taking a very high-level view of the information risk management concepts and relationships between them.

Figure 0.1 illustrates the interrelationships between seven key areas of information risk management. We will expand on the individual concepts in due course, but for now it is worthwhile keeping this picture in mind as we work through the remaining chapters of this book.

DEFINITIONS

Asset – 'any item that has value to the organisation' (ISO/IEC 27000:2012). Assets can be tangible, such as buildings, systems, people or information, or intangible, such as brand or reputation. Intellectual property (IP) is also an asset and results from the expression of an idea. IP might be a patent, trademark, copyright, design right, registered design, technical or commercial information. Bizarrely, although IP can be owned, bought and sold, information per se is not considered 'property' in the strictest sense of UK law.

Attack – 'an aggressive action against a person, an organisation or an asset intended to cause damage or loss' (ISO/IEC 27000:2014). An attack can be a simple event, such

Figure 0.1 Concepts and relationships

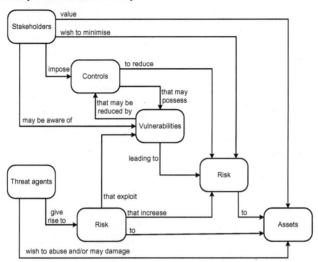

as an attempt to break into a computer system, or a more complex event such as a distributed denial of service (DDoS) attack in which multiple systems mount an attack on an information asset. Attacks differ slightly from threats and hazards in that attacks are something that actually happen, whereas threats and hazards only have the potential to cause harm. An attacker is therefore someone who deliberately sets out to cause harm. See also exploit.

Communication and consultation – 'the continual and iterative processes that an organisation conducts to provide, share or obtain information, and to engage in dialogue with stakeholders regarding the management of risk' (ISO Guide 73:2009). Such dialogue will be with internal stakeholders, such as senior managers and staff involved in managing information, and also external stakeholders such as outsourcing organisations.

Communication and consultation must happen continuously throughout the lifecycle (and beyond) of an information risk management project or programme of work, and must never be viewed as a one-off exercise; and it should be remembered that communication and consultation is a two-way process.

Consequence or impact – 'an outcome of an event affecting objectives' (ISO Guide 73:2009). The two terms are both widely used and are completely interchangeable. Consequences and impacts may be direct, for example the loss of a building due to a fire, or indirect, such as the fine imposed for a breach of the Data Protection Act.

Also, there are primary impacts, such as the loss of revenue when a system fails, and secondary impacts such as the overtime payments to staff for working extra hours to repair or replace such a system.

As we shall see later in this book, consequences and impact may be described in a qualitative or a quantitative manner. Qualitative descriptions are generally in the form of 'trivial', 'minor', 'major', 'severe' or 'critical', but unless they are based on some form of numerical value, do not really provide an insightful assessment of the grim reality.

Quantitative descriptions are much easier to understand and provide a firm basis for comparison and assessment, but are generally much harder to predict with any accuracy unless very detailed analysis is carried out, which can be time consuming.

In practice, the best balance can usually be obtained by providing a quantitative rating for a qualitative term, for example: between £1 million and £10 million represents 'severe', which allows a greater degree of subjectivity whilst anchoring the assessment in numeric terms. This is sometimes referred to as a semi-quantitative measure.

Context establishment – 'defining the external and internal parameters to be taken into account when managing risk, and setting the scope and risk criteria for the risk management policy' (ISO Guide 73:2009). This is discussed in greater detail in Chapter 3.

Control – 'a measure that is modifying risk' (ISO Guide 73:2009). Controls can be strategic, tactical or operational. Strategic controls are very high level, such as risk avoidance, transfer, reduction and acceptance. Tactical controls determine a general course of action, such as detective, preventative, corrective and directive Operational controls determine the actual treatment, such as technical or logical, procedural or people and physical or environmental.

Cyber security refers specifically to information security as applied to computers, tablet computers, smartphones, computer networks (both public and private) and the wider Internet. In this respect it is slightly different from the wider area of information security, which includes non-electronic information as well. Cyber security is sometimes also referred to as computer security or IT security.

Disruption – this term is generally applied to events or incidents that interfere with normal business operations and have a detrimental impact on information or information processing.

Estimation – it is almost impossible to predict either the impact or the likelihood of a threat arising with any degree of accuracy or certainty, so almost all risk assessments are carried out on the basis of estimation. Estimates can be refined and improved over time, and with the hindsight of real events they may even become quite accurate, but initially they will always be little more than an educated guess.

Event – 'the occurrence or change of a particular set of circumstances' (ISO Guide 73:2009). Sometimes these are referred to as incidents, and whilst there are similarities, there needs to be a differentiation between the various types of change of circumstances.

In terms of information risk, events can vary considerably in scale and severity from so-called 'glitches', lasting perhaps a fraction of a second, through to major incidents that can affect the organisation for weeks or months. In order to place events in a clearer descriptive context, examples are provided in Chapter 4.

Exploit – an exploit is a particular form of attack in which a tried and tested method of causing impact is followed with some rigour. Exploits are similar in nature to processes, but whereas processes are generally benign, exploits are almost always harmful.

External context – 'the external environment in which the organisation seeks to achieve its objectives' (ISO Guide 73:2009). Again, as the name suggests, the external context takes in factors outside the bounds of the organisation. This is discussed in greater detail in Chapter 3.

Frequency – 'the number of events or outcomes per defined unit of time. Note: Frequency can be applied to past events or to potential future events, where it can be used as a measure of likelihood or probability' (ISO Guide 73:2009). Most real-world events are not precisely regular in occurrence – the tides and phases of the moon being obvious exceptions– and so any statements of frequency are only really estimates and cannot be relied upon for accuracy.

Hazard – 'a source of potential harm' (ISO Guide 73:2009). Hazards are generally seen as natural (as opposed to manufactured) events, such as flooding, hurricanes or ice storms. See also Threats.

Information assurance – is the process of ensuring that data is not lost when critical events or incidents occur. It is generally associated with computer, cyber or IT security rather than the somewhat wider meaning of 'information security'.

Information security – is the practice of protecting information from unauthorised access, use, disclosure, disruption, modification or destruction. Information security encompasses both physical and electronic information.

Internal context – 'the internal environment in which the organisation seeks to achieve its objectives' (ISO Guide 73:2009). As the name suggests, the internal context is that which exists within the organisation itself. This is discussed in greater detail in Chapter 3.

Likelihood – 'the chance of something happening' (ISO Guide 73:2009). The terms 'likelihood' and 'probability' are often used interchangeably, but likelihood is a rather general or qualitative term denoting a degree of uncertainty, whereas the quantitative term, probability, has a more statistical underpinning. The term 'possibility' is generally not used, since many things are possible, and the term gives no indication whether or not the event is actually likely to take place.

Probability – 'the measure of the chance of occurrence expressed as a number between zero and one, where zero is impossibility and one is absolute certainty' (ISO Guide 73:2009). Probability is often expressed as a percentage, and being a quantitative term, is able to express the chance of something happening with a greater degree of accuracy. See also Likelihood.

Processes and procedures – many organisations do not think of processes as being information assets, but as they are documented in some way and often refer to the use or production of information, they can be considered as intangible assets. Processes detail how to go about achieving a goal or objective. Procedures, which are a subset of processes, explain how to conduct the individual steps within processes, and therefore take on the same status as intangible assets.

Qualitative risk assessments – these are subjective in nature, and are generally expressed in verbal terms such as 'high', 'medium' and 'low'. This is not an ideal state of affairs, as it renders risk assessments unreliable, and should be grounded in more rigorously. This is discussed in greater detail in Chapter 4.

Quantitative risk assessment – these are objective in nature and are generally expressed in numerical terms, such as financial values, percentages and so on. Whilst these provide a more accurate measurement of risk, they are usually more time consuming to undertake. They are discussed in greater detail in Chapter 4.

Residual risk – 'the risk remaining after risk treatment' (ISO Guide 73:2009). Once all other risk treatment options have been explored, it is often the case that some (usually small) risk remains. It is normal to accept or tolerate this, since further treatment might either have no effect, or might be prohibitively expensive. Because residual risks are often very small, they are occasionally (incorrectly) overlooked.

Resilience – the 'adaptive capacity of an organisation in a complex and changing environment' (ISO Guide 73:2009). Although this definition refers to organisations rather than to information assets, the definition holds true, in that where an information asset is properly protected, it is able to resist certain threats. However, to make an information asset fully resilient may be a very complex task and require several different methods of protection.

Risk – 'the effect of uncertainty on objectives' (ISO Guide 73:2009). Risk is the product of consequence or impact and likelihood or probability, and is not the same as a threat or hazard. In the context of information risk management, risk is usually taken to have negative connotations. In the wider context of risk, however, it can also bee seen in a positive light and referred to as 'opportunity'.

Risk acceptance or risk tolerance – 'the informed decision to take a particular risk' (ISO Guide 73:2009). Risk acceptance or tolerance is the final choice in risk treatment once all other possible avenues have been explored. This is not the same as ignoring risks – something that should never be done.

Risk aggregation – 'the combination of a number of risks into one risk to develop a more complete understanding of the overall risk' (ISO Guide 73:2009). Where a number of risks exist in a certain area, it may be possible to treat them all with one or more controls rather than treating them individually. Therefore, for the purposes of risk management, they can be grouped together or aggregated in order to save time and effort.

Risk analysis – 'the process to comprehend the nature of risk and to determine the level of risk' (ISO Guide 73:2009). This is the part where we combine the impact and the likelihood (or probability) to calculate the level of risk and to plot it onto a risk matrix, which allows us to compare risks for their severity and to decide which are in greatest need of treatment.

Risk appetite – 'the amount and type of risk that an organisation is willing to pursue or retain' (ISO Guide 73:2009). Organisations will have differing levels of risk appetite for different types of information; and different types of organisation will have vastly differing levels of risk appetite, depending on their sector.

Risk assessment – 'the overall process of risk identification, risk analysis and risk evaluation' (ISO Guide 73:2009). It includes identification of the information assets and their owners; impact assessment; threat and vulnerability identification; likelihood assessment; risk analysis; production of the risk matrix; and, finally, risk evaluation.

Risk avoidance or risk termination – 'an informed decision not to be involved in, or to withdraw from, an activity in order not to be exposed to a particular risk' (ISO Guide 73:2009). This is one of the four strategic options for risk treatment. Avoiding the risk should normally remove the risk completely, but may leave the organisation with other challenges.

Risk criteria – 'the terms of reference against which the significance of a risk is evaluated' (ISO Guide 73:2009). Risk criteria will include such things as impact, likelihood, proximity and risk appetite.

Risk evaluation – 'the process of comparing the results of risk analysis with risk criteria to determine whether the risk and/or its magnitude is acceptable or tolerable' (ISO Guide 73:2009). This is the final stage in the risk assessment process, in which all risks plotted onto the risk matrix are evaluated against a set of criteria in order to decide which should receive the highest priority for treatment.

Risk identification – 'the process of finding, recognising and describing risks' (ISO Guide 73:2009). Risk identification includes the identification risk sources, events, their causes and the possible consequences to the information assets.

Risk management – 'coordinated activities to direct and control an organisation with regard to risk' (ISO Guide 73:2009). Risk management is the identification, assessment and prioritisation of risks (defined in ISO 31000 as the effect of uncertainty on objectives, whether positive or negative) followed by coordinated and economical application of resources to minimise, monitor and control the probability and/or impact of unfortunate events or to maximise the realisation of opportunities.

Risk modification or risk reduction – the process of treating risk by the use of controls to reduce either the consequence/impact or the likelihood/probability. Sometimes the term 'risk treatment' is used in this context, but risk treatment is really a generic term for all four kinds of strategic control. Strangely, ISO Guide 73 does not attempt to define risk modification or reduction, although it does refer to it under the definition of 'control'.

Risk monitoring – 'the continual checking, supervising, critically observing or determining the status in order to identify change from the performance level required or expected' (ISO Guide 73:2009). This is an ongoing process to ensure that risks that change over time – whether for the better or the worse – are reviewed and that appropriate action is taken.

Risk proximity – how far away in time the risk will occur (if it materialises). It can also mean: when will the risk occur? Whilst there does not appear to be a Standards definition for risk proximity, it remains a vital element of the risk assessment process, since those risks that could manifest themselves sooner will probably require attention before those that are further away in time. Risk proximity is one of the criteria against which risks are evaluated.

Risk register – 'a record of information about identified risks' (ISO Guide 73:2009). Simple risk registers are often maintained as a spreadsheet, whilst more complex registers may use a proprietary software package capable not only of recording the information but also of carrying out some analysis or evaluation.

Risk retention – 'the acceptance of the potential benefit of gain, or burden of loss, from a particular risk' (ISO Guide 73:2009). Once risks have undergone the risk treatment process, there may be some outstanding risk that cannot be further reduced, transferred or eliminated. This is referred to as 'residual risk', and risk retention is the ongoing process of managing this.

Risk review – 'the activity undertaken to determine the suitability, adequacy and effectiveness of the subject matter to achieve established objectives' (ISO Guide 73:2009). Risk reviews capture not only that of the risks and their treatments, but also the whole process by which risk management is undertaken, the status of information assets and the organisation's risk appetite.

Risk tolerance – 'an organisation or stakeholder's readiness to bear the risk after risk treatment in order to achieve its objectives' (ISO Guide 73:2009). Risk tolerance is sometimes also viewed as being the same as risk acceptance. The difference is that risk acceptance takes place when no other form of risk treatment is suitable, whereas risk tolerance takes place after other forms of risk treatment have taken place, and there is some residual risk.

Risk transference or risk sharing – 'a form of risk treatment involving the agreed distribution of risk with other parties' (ISO Guide 73:2009). One of the risk treatment options is to transfer the risk to or to share it with a third party. Transferring or sharing the risk, however, does not change ownership of the risk, which remains with the organisation itself, regardless of who else shares the risk.

Risk treatment – 'the process to modify risk' (ISO Guide 73:2009). Whilst this may be technically correct, treatment may alternatively involve risk transference or sharing, or risk avoidance or termination. Risk modification or reduction is generally viewed as one of the methods of treating risk.

Stakeholder – 'a person or organisation that can affect, be affected by, or perceive themselves to be affected by a decision or activity' (ISO Guide 73:2009). Stakeholders may be people within or outside the organisation, including customers, suppliers or Government.

Threat – 'a potential cause of an unwanted incident, which may result in harm to a system or organisation' (ISO/IEC 27000:2014). ISO Guide 73 defines 'hazards', but does not refer to threats. Whilst hazards are generally viewed as natural events, threats are usually manufactured, whether accidental or deliberate.

Threat actors and threat sources – a threat source is a person or organisation that wishes to benefit from attacking an information asset. A threat actor is a person or organisation that actually mounts the attack. Threat sources often pressurise threat actors to attack information assets on their behalf.

Threat vectors – the method or mechanism by which an attack is launched against an information asset.

Uncertainty – 'this is the state, even partial, of deficiency of information related to, understanding or knowledge of, an event, its consequence, or likelihood' (ISO Guide 73:2009). Whilst not an actual term defined in the Guide, uncertainty is explained in a note below the definition of risk. Uncertainty goes hand-in-hand with estimation, meaning that many of our assessments will be subject to a greater or lesser degree of uncertainty. In some cases, uncertainty increases as a possible event's proximity decreases.

Vulnerability – 'the intrinsic properties of something resulting in susceptibility to a risk source that can lead to an event with a consequence' (ISO Guide 73:2009). Vulnerabilities or weaknesses in or surrounding an asset leave it open to attack from a threat or hazard. Vulnerabilities come in two flavours: intrinsic vulnerabilities, which are something inherent in the very nature of an information asset, such as the ease of erasing information from magnetic media (whether accidental or deliberate); and extrinsic vulnerabilities are those that are poorly applied, such as software that is out-of-date due to a lack of patching.

INFORMATION RISK MANAGEMENT STANDARDS

There are a number of useful standards and guidelines available to risk management practitioners. Unfortunately, the BS, ISO and AS/NZS standards can only be purchased, although members of BSI enjoy a discount on many standards. The NIST and CNSS standards are free to download.

The following list includes only the most relevant standards. For a fuller list of all related standards, please see Appendix H.

British Standards Institute (BSI)

https://bsol.bsigroup.com

BS 7799-3:2006 *Information security management systems – Guidelines for information security risk management*

BS 31100:2011 *Risk management – Code of practice and guidance for the implementation of BS ISO 31000*

International Standards Organisation (ISO)

http://www.iso.org/iso/home/standards.htm

ISO Guide 73:2009 *Risk management – Vocabulary*

ISO/IEC 27000:2014 *Information technology – Security techniques – Information security management systems – Overview and vocabulary*

ISO/IEC 27001:2013 *Information technology – Security techniques – Information Security Management Systems – Requirements*

ISO/IEC 27002:2013 *Information technology – Security techniques – Code of practice for information security management*

ISO/IEC 27005:2011 *Information technology – Security techniques – Information security risk management*

ISO 31000:2009 *Risk management – Principles and guidelines*

IEC 31010:2009 *Risk management – Risk assessment techniques*

US National Institute of Standards and Technology

http://csrc.nist.gov/publications/PubsSPs.html

NIST SP 800-30 Revision 1, September 2012 *Guide for conducting risk assessments*

US Committee on National Security Systems (CNSS)

http://www.ncix.gov/publications/policy/

CNSS Instruction No. 4009 26 April 2010 *National information assurance (IA) glossary*

Australia/New Zealand Standards

http://www.standards.org.au

AS/NZS 4360:2004 *Risk management*

UK Institute of Risk Management

http://www.theirm.org/

The Risk Management Standard (2002)

Federation of European Risk Management Associations

http://www.ferma.eu/risk-management/standards/

Risk Management Standard (2003)

Information Security Forum (ISF)

https://www.securityforum.org

The Standard of Good Practice for Information Security (2013) – Area SR1 – Information Risk Assessment

GLOSSARY OF TERMS

The following definitions relate to the list of standards given at the end of this Glossary, with corresponding number from the list given in square brackets. A few are not defined in any standards, and are suggestions.

Access control The means to ensure that access to assets is authorised and restricted on business and security requirements [1]

Asset Any item that has value to the organisation [4]

Attack An attempt to destroy, expose, alter, disable, steal or gain unauthorised access to or make unauthorised use of an asset [1]

Attribute The property or characteristic of an object that can be distinguished quantitatively or qualitatively by human or automated means [1]

Audit The systematic, independent and documented process for obtaining audit evidence and evaluating it objectively to determine the extent to which the audit criteria are fulfilled [1]

Authentication The provision of assurance that a claimed characteristic of an entity is correct [1]

Availability Property of being accessible and usable upon demand by an authorised entity [1]

Business continuity (BC) The capability of the organisation to continue delivery of products and services at acceptable pre-defined levels following a disruptive incident [2]

Business impact analysis (BIA) The process of analysing activities and the effect that a business disruption might have upon them [2]

Communication and consultation The continual and iterative processes that an organisation conducts to provide, share or obtain information, and to engage in dialogue with stakeholders regarding the management of risk [3]

Confidentiality The property that information is not made available or disclosed to unauthorised individuals, entities or processes [1]

Consequence An outcome of an event affecting objectives [3]

Context establishment Defining the external and internal parameters to be taken into account when managing risk, and setting the scope and risk criteria for the risk management policy [3]

Control A measure that is modifying risk [3]

Control objective A statement describing what is to be achieved as a result of implementing controls [1]

Data A collection of values assigned to base measures, derived measures and/or indicators [1]

Disaster recovery (DR) A coordinated activity to enable the recovery of ICT systems and networks due to a disruption

Effectiveness The extent to which planned activities are realised and planned results achieved [1]

Event The occurrence or change of a particular set of circumstances [3]

Exposure The extent to which an organisation and/or stakeholder is subject to an event [3]

External context The external environment in which the organisation seeks to achieve its objectives [1]

Hazard A source of potential harm [3]

Horizon scanning A procedure that involves the systematic observation and monitoring of various key drivers of change at the margins of current thinking and planning

Impact An outcome of an event affecting objectives

Information An organised and formatted collection of data

Information security The preservation of confidentiality, integrity and availability of information [1]

Information security event An information security event is an identified occurrence of a system, service or network state indicating a possible breach of information security policy or failure of safeguards, or a previously unknown situation that may be security relevant [1]

Information security incident An information security incident is indicated by a single or a series of unwanted or unexpected information security events that have a significant probability of compromising business operations and threatening information security [1]

Inherent risk The risk that an activity would pose if no controls or other mitigating factors were in place (the gross risk or risk before controls) [5]

Integrity Property of protecting the accuracy and completeness of assets [1]

Internal context The internal environment in which the organisation seeks to achieve its objectives [3]

Level of risk The magnitude of a risk expressed in terms of the combination of consequences and their likelihood [1]

Likelihood The chance of something happening [3]

Monitoring Determining the status of a system, a process or an activity [2]

Non-repudiation The ability to prove the occurrence of a claimed event or action and its originating entities, in order to resolve disputes about the occurrence or non-occurrence of the event or action and involvement of entities in the event [1]

Objective A result to be achieved [1]

Organisation A person or group of people that has its own functions with responsibilities, authorities and relationships to achieve its objectives [1]

Outsource Make an arrangement where an external organisation performs part of an organisation's function or process [1]

Policy The intentions of an organisation as formally expressed by its top management [1]

Probability The measure of the chance of occurrence expressed as a number between 0 and 1, where 0 is impossibility and 1 is absolute certainty [3]

Process A set of interacting activities, which transforms inputs into outputs [1]

Qualitative risk assessment Mostly entirely subjective and therefore less accurate than quantitative risk assessments. However, their benefit is that they are much quicker to produce than the quantitative kind

Quantitative risk assessment If conducted with rigour, these produce very accurate results and are extremely objective. The downside of this approach is that accurate data is needed to begin with, and it can be very time consuming

Requirement The need or expectation that is stated, generally implied or obligatory [1]

Residual risk The risk remaining after risk treatment [3]

Review An activity undertaken to determine the suitability, adequacy and effectiveness of the subject matter to achieve established objectives [1]

Risk The effect of uncertainty on objectives [3]

Risk acceptance The informed decision to take a particular risk [3]

Risk aggregation The combination of a number of risks into one risk to develop a more complete understanding of the overall risk [3]

Risk analysis The process to comprehend the nature of risk and to determine the level of risk [3]

Risk appetite The amount and type of risk that an organisation is willing to pursue or retain [3]

Risk assessment The overall process of risk identification, risk analysis and risk evaluation [3]

Risk aversion The attitude to turn away from risk [3]

Risk avoidance An informed decision not to be involved in, or to withdraw from, an activity in order not to be exposed to a particular risk [3]

Risk criteria The terms of reference against which the significance of a risk is evaluated [3]

Risk evaluation The process of comparing the results of risk analysis with risk criteria to determine whether the risk and/or its magnitude is acceptable or tolerable [3]

Risk identification The process of finding, recognising and describing risks [3]

Risk management The coordinated activities to direct and control an organisation with regard to risk [3]

Risk matrix A graphical representation of impact versus likelihood used to assist in the prioritisation of risks

Risk modification The process of treating risk by the use of controls to reduce either the consequence/impact or the likelihood/probability

Risk monitoring The continual checking, supervising, critically observing or determining the status in order to identify change from the performance level required or expected [3]

Risk owner A person or entity with the accountability and authority to manage a risk [3]

Risk proximity How far away in time the risk will occur (if it materialises). It can also mean: when will the risk occur?

Risk reduction The process of treating risk by the use of controls to reduce either the consequence/impact or the likelihood/probability

Risk register A record of information about identified risks [3]

Risk reporting A form of communication intended to inform particular internal or external stakeholders by providing information regarding the current state of risk and its management [3]

Risk retention The acceptance of the potential benefit of gain, or burden of loss, from a particular risk [3]

Risk review The activity undertaken to determine the suitability, adequacy and effectiveness of the subject matter to achieve established objectives [3]

Risk sharing A form of risk treatment involving the agreed distribution of risk with other parties [3]

Risk termination An informed decision not to be involved in, or to withdraw from, an activity in order not to be exposed to a particular risk

Risk tolerance An organisation's or stakeholder's readiness to bear the risk after risk treatment in order to achieve its objectives [3]

Risk transfer A form of risk treatment involving the agreed distribution of risk with other parties

Risk treatment The process to modify risk [3]

Scale An ordered set of values, continuous or discrete, or a set of categories to which the attribute is mapped [1]

Stakeholder A person or organisation that can affect, be affected by or perceive themselves to be affected by a decision or activity [3]

Threat The potential cause of an unwanted incident, which may result in harm to a system or organisation [1]

Validation Confirmation, through the provision of objective evidence, that the requirements for a specific intended use or application have been fulfilled [1]

Verification Confirmation, through the provision of objective evidence, that specified requirements have been fulfilled [1]

Vulnerability The intrinsic properties of something resulting in susceptibility to a risk source that can lead to an event with a consequence [3]

SOURCES OF STANDARDS INFORMATION

1. ISO/IEC 27000:2014 *Information technology – Security techniques – Information security management systems – Overview and vocabulary*
2. ISO 22300:2012 *Societal security – Business continuity management systems – Requirements*
3. ISO Guide 73:2009 *Risk management – Vocabulary*
4. ISO/IEC 27000:2012 *Information technology – Security techniques – Information security management systems – Overview and vocabulary*
5. *The Information Security Handbook*. Available at: http://ishandbook.bsewall.com/risk/Assess/Risk/inherent_risk.html

PREFACE

When it has become known that I have been writing this book, people say, 'Oh, I see. It's all about computer security then.' Actually, no, it isn't. Certainly computer security appears very frequently in many sections of the book – this is quite natural, since much of the information on which we rely today is either generated by, accessed through or stored on a computer system of some description.

In fact, most of the underlying issues are caused by people who have not been properly trained to do their job, who have not done it correctly or who are simply unaware that there was anything for them to do in the first place.

Technology is frequently the tool we use to secure information as well as to generate and store it and these activities are easily interchanged in people's minds, resulting in confusion and misinterpretation. After all, if you leave your car unlocked and your mobile phone, wallet or laptop are stolen, it is not the car's fault is it?

It is time we stopped blaming technology for all our woes, and concentrated instead in understanding not only what is happening, but also, and more importantly, why it is happening. Then and only then we can do something positive about it and prevent it from recurring.

For more than ten years now, I have been delivering an annual lecture on business continuity at the Royal Holloway, University of London. The lecture is part of their MSc course in Information Security and generally takes place in December, by which time the first-year students have been on campus for about two months.

Before I begin my talk, I ask them, 'What do you think information security is really about?' The answers vary – usually confidentiality, integrity and availability are mentioned, and occasionally terms like 'cyber security' are put forward.

My belief, and what I then go on to say, is that information security is actually all about the management of information risk, and that everything they learn on the course is about identifying and prioritising those risks, taking actions to prevent them from occurring, knowing if and when they do occur, reducing or halting the impact of their occurring and, where appropriate, knowingly and objectively accepting the consequences.

It does not actually matter whether the information is in physical or electronic form; what matters is that it is important to someone and therefore warrants protection from theft, exposure or abuse.

It is an unfortunate fact of life that we do not always value things until they are lost. This is especially true of information. Were the last digits of someone's telephone number 674 or 647? Does a colleague live at number 24 or number 42?

Whilst these are trivial examples of the loss or misunderstanding of information, they serve to illustrate how dependent we are on information of all kinds, but they fall short of recognising the effects of information either being permanently lost or (possibly worse), falling into the wrong hands.

In recent months, there have been numerous reports in the media about how the security services, particularly in the UK and the USA are intercepting communications. Whilst this in itself is laudable in the fight against international terrorism – it is, after all, their primary role – it is clear that some governments, organisations and people have different objectives, and are seeking to mine our information in order to use it for their commercial, financial or political gain at our expense.

The general principles we use to protect our information can be found in *Information Security Management Principles* (second edition, published by BCS, The Chartered Institute for IT, ISBN 948-1-78017-175-3), Chapter 2 of which deals with information risk. However, this is only an 18-page summary account of the subject, and therefore only scratches the surface.

The lesson – as many a security professional will tell you – is that if a well-resourced opponent really wants to read your information, steal it or change it, then they will find a way of doing so. It may not be cheap or easy, it may involve using a mix of technology and human agents, but if they have sufficient motivation, you will find it very, very hard to stop them.

The intention of this book is therefore to help you to make life as difficult as possible for them to be successful.

Throughout the book, you will see icons in the margins to guide you to important information in the text. Here is the key:

ANECDOTE

An anecdote or case study: real-life experiences from information risk managers who have been there.

1 THE NEED FOR INFORMATION RISK MANAGEMENT

INTRODUCTION

Before we begin to study further the need for information risk management, let us take a look at a few case studies to illustrate instances in which information was accessed or used inappropriately.

CASE STUDY 1

The hacker finished his coffee, checked the code one last time, and pressed the 'execute' button. As the egg-timer icon appeared on his computer screen, he turned out the light and went to bed. The computer churned away for hours whilst he slept, and finally flashed a 'completed' message on the screen.

It had taken him several hours to write the code, but he had finally succeeded. His first task was to search an Internet website for a list of the most popular names in the UK. This took less than five minutes, revealed 500 men's and women's forenames and almost 1,400 surnames.

The program took each forename and surname in turn and placed them together as a string, so 'john' and 'smith' became 'johnsmith', and then for good measure added a second combination with dot between them, as in 'john.smith'. The program then added each of 20 of the most popular email suffixes to each combination, which provided a total list of 55 million possible email addresses.

He had toyed briefly with the idea of creating 'johnasmith' and 'john.a.smith' combinations as well, but decided to leave this for another day and to see how the first batch fared.

He had carefully studied every spam email he had received, seen the obvious grammatical and spelling mistakes they had made, and had crafted his message with precise attention to detail. The typeface, text size and colour was identical to that used by a major UK banking group; their logo was copied from their own website and pasted into the message; the language was carefully chosen, and he was sure that there was nothing in the message text that would arouse suspicion.

Next, using a number of Hotmail accounts, the program began sending out its messages. So as not to trigger alarms on the ISPs' systems, it changed sending accounts randomly, transmitted to just 20 addresses at a time, all in the blind copy or 'bcc' field, and using a very carefully chosen 'from' address.

The email invited the recipient to click on the hyperlink at the end of the message to confirm their bank account number, sort code and password. If they did so, the website to which they connected – another computer in the hacker's house – would record this information and then transmit an email thanking the customer and reassuring them that their account was fully in order and that their banking details were safely stored.

Both facts were true. The customer's account was perfectly in order, and the hacker was securely storing their details!

He knew that if only one per cent of the email addresses the program had generated was genuine, over half a million people would receive the message; if only one per cent of those actually had an account with that particular bank, more than 5,000 customers would consider responding; and if only one per cent of those actually responded, he would have more than 50 complete sets of banking details.

Did that represent a small return on investment? Maybe, but when you consider what the hacker could achieve with those bank details in terms of fraud, the amount of time he had invested in research and development was well worth the potential return, and this was just one hacker, and just one night's work.

The risks he faced were very low. If his messages caused an ISP to block one of the many Hotmail accounts, he would simply acquire others. The Internet address to which the target customers might respond would only be active for a few days before he removed it – just long enough to gain valuable information; not long enough to attract too much attention.

In one sense, the example I have given here is pure fiction. It was written simply to illustrate the point that there are people 'out there' who want to obtain information and are eminently capable of doing so. The specific methods my fictional hacker used may or may not be entirely accurate, but the principles are, and it only takes a one in a million success rate to get lucky.

 CASE STUDY 2

The head of marketing had a temporary personal assistant working for her whilst her usual assistant was on maternity leave. The temp had worked for the organisation several times already in the past and was familiar with the way the organisation worked and who did what.

The organisation's monthly newsletter was to be sent out by email to their whole client base, and the assistant was delegated to action this. He carefully proofread the newsletter, checked the email list and brought the two together.

It was not until a day or so later that the head of marketing realised that, instead of using the 'blind carbon copy', or 'bcc', field to add the mailing list, the assistant had used the 'to' field and every one of the organisation's clients could now see the email addresses of all the others.

This is a very simple error – it has happened many times, is easily made, but is difficult to recover from. The organisation received a number of emails of complaint from aggrieved clients, but managed to come through the incident with their reputation reasonably intact. The assistant subsequently received training on the procedures for this kind of activity, and the head of marketing learnt a valuable lesson in not making unwarranted assumptions about the level of knowledge or ability of staff, temporary or permanent.

CASE STUDY 3

A cancer specialist was asked to act as an expert witness in a case where a claim of negligence had been made against a surgeon. The specialist's assistant emailed the full details of the case, including the patient's previous medical history, the notes made before and after the failed operation, and the surgeon's statement together with the specialist's written evidence and commentary, back to the legal firm who were prosecuting the case.

Unfortunately the assistant did not check the recipient's email address prior to pressing 'send', and the whole set of documentation was emailed to someone entirely different.

At this point, because the email contained what the Data Protection Act (DPA) refers to as 'sensitive personal data', the line between 'unfortunate mistake' and 'negligence' was crossed.

The recipient was in a position to carry out several possible courses of action:

First, he could have made the Information Commissioner aware of the error, which may well have resulted in serious consequences for both the assistant and her employer. Second, he could have contacted the surgeon and advised him of the specialist's comments, which would almost certainly have jeopardised the case against him.

In fact, the recipient contacted the specialist's assistant, advised her of the error and deleted the original email, thus avoiding several catastrophes.

Most readers of this book will have their own horror stories to relate. In the instance of the third case study, the author was the recipient of the unintended email, and even subsequently received several others relating to the same cancer specialist. Although this has now been remedied, there have been several other similar examples where the author's email address is similar to that of the intended recipients, and in each case a polite response has been sent, followed by deletion of the offending email, but the problem still persists.

Is everyone who receives such emails as diligent, or do some of them make use of the information they receive to their own ends or to the detriment of the intended recipient? Readers must decide for themselves what they would think and how they would feel if the email attachments contained their own medical records, financial statements, formulae or designs.

WHAT IS INFORMATION?

Before we begin to examine the need for information risk management, it is important to understand what the difference is between information and data.

Superficially, this appears to be quite straightforward – data are merely unstructured facts and figures, whereas information consists of data that are organised into a meaningful context. For example, the temperature, wind speed and direction, rainfall and atmospheric pressure readings taken twice daily in towns and cities around the country are just data. It is only when they are recorded along with yesterday's readings and those of previous days that the data are placed in context and begin to have meaning, allowing meteorologists to examine trends and develop a weather forecast. It is at this point that the data have become organised and structured and can now be seen as information.

Although I have drawn the distinction between the two, for the purposes of this book I shall deal with them both under the heading of 'information', since both data and information will have value to their owners and must be equally protected, although the owner of the original data and the owner of the resulting information may be entirely different entities.

Information can exist in two different states: physical, with information recorded on paper, canvas or even pieces of clay with cuneiform indentations and notches in tally sticks; and electronic, with binary ones and zeros stored on magnetic media or other types of memory device.

Information also comes in two distinct forms. First, there is information that describes or lists other information, such as a catalogue or index, and is often referred to as 'metadata'. Second, there is information that is something in its own right, such as a novel, a software application or the formula for a new medicinal drug. All have value to their owner or originator, and indeed may either be of a personal nature, in which case will be subject to data protection legislation, or may be Intellectual Property (IP), in which case copyright or trademark legislation will apply.

It is not the author's intention to deal in any depth with either of these two aspects of legislation since each could easily be the subject of a book in its own right, but the reader should be aware not only of their existence and general content, but also that they need to be taken into account when developing an information risk management programme.

Recent revelations regarding the organised interception and mining of information by various security agencies have raised awareness at all levels of society of the need to take greater care of our information, but should we be surprised by the extent to which this so-called 'snooping' takes place, or by the fact that these agencies are able to carry it out?

The problem lies in the distinction between the need to maintain national security and the need to gather sufficient information to be able to do so. Security agencies such as the NSA in America and GCHQ in the UK were set up precisely to carry out this kind of work, so it should not come as a shock to anybody that they are doing it, nor that they are very successful at doing so, albeit subject to strict legal undertakings, at least in theory. What should be more worrying is that other nations' security agencies may be able to undertake similar surveillance and interception and may use the resulting information gathered for nefarious purposes.

Then there is the question of so-called 'Big Data', in which organisations – both commercial and governmental – collect vast amounts of information on us as individuals. Every time we use a credit card to purchase goods, the credit card agency gathers a little more information about us. This has positive benefits as well as negative connotations; for example, if a transaction falls outside your 'normal' spending profile, the credit card agency can contact you to verify that your card is still in your possession and has not been used fraudulently.

On the other hand, of course, supermarkets may target us with advertising and promotions as a result of aggregating information gained from our loyalty cards, which may or may not be something to be happy about since they now know more about our spending habits than perhaps we do.

Whatever the situation, we sometimes do not treat our own or other people's information with sufficient care, and the consequences of this can be severe. When scaled up from a personal to an organisational level, the consequences can be catastrophic, and it is hoped that this book will enable the reader to take a proactive position in preventing this from happening.

Finally, we should make the distinction between information that is about what we do, and information about who we are. Information about what we do could cover such things as where we spend our money, what our audio and visual entertainment preferences are, what we view on the Internet, what we say online and anything that can be recorded about actions we have undertaken.

Information about who we are will include those so-called immutable attributes. These are absolute facts and can never be altered. They include such things as our biological parents, our biometrics (e.g. iris scan, fingerprints or DNA), where and when we were born.

Next, there are so-called assigned attributes such as our nationality, names, national insurance number or title. These are generally the attributes that people and organisations rely upon to identify and communicate with us, and rarely change.

Finally, there are other related attributes, which, whilst being a part of our personae, are more easily changed, but still allow people and organisations to identify and communicate with us, and which may be used in identity verification, such as usernames and passwords, email addresses, memberships, qualifications and entitlements.

Many of these types of information are almost impossible to conceal since they are a matter of public record and we are happy to make them available – indeed, it is often in our interests to do so, although there are some that we would naturally not make publicly available. For example, we are usually happy to give someone our email address, but at the same time we would not let them know the password to the email account.

THE INFORMATION LIFE CYCLE

It is easy to imagine that information is 'just there', but it must be created in the first place, and then generally follows a set path as shown in Figure 1.1.

Figure 1.1 The information lifecycle

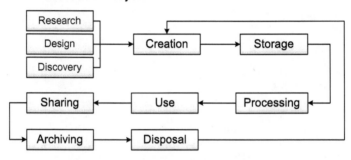

The creative process begins with some form of research, design or discovery which allows the creator to record the information in some form, whether in hard copy or electronic form, and then to store it in some way.

In some situations, the information may be processed either to manipulate it in a way so that others can easily access it or to make it more useful by enriching it in some way.

The process continues with use, either by the information's creator alone, or, more frequently, by others, whether individually or collaboratively, at which point it can be widely shared either within a confined environment or publicly.

At some stage, the information may become out of date, but may still be required as a time-based reference, in which case it will be archived. Eventually, the information will become completely redundant, at which point it can safely be disposed of or destroyed, or it may be updated and recycled as new information.

At each stage of this lifecycle process, there will be the need to ensure that the information is adequately protected from accidental or deliberate loss, change or destruction, hence the need for information risk management.

WHO SHOULD USE INFORMATION RISK MANAGEMENT?

Quite simply, any part of an organisation can and should make use of information risk management, since all parts of an organisation are likely to have information that has value to the organisation.

Human Resources keep records of personnel, much of which will be considered to be personal information under the DPA; Sales and Marketing departments will hold information on past and projected sales as well as pricing schedules; Finance will hold records of the organisation's income and expenditure; Development will have plans and designs for both current and future products and services; the IT department, although perhaps not owning any of this information, will be responsible for keeping it secure and making it available to authorised staff.

Non-commercial organisations too will have valuable information that must be protected. Hospitals, GP practices and health trusts hold sensitive personal information on patients; local authorities hold lists of vulnerable people; the Driver and Licensing Authority holds details of every driver and vehicle registered in the UK; and Her Majesty's Revenue and Customs hold huge amounts of financial information about every taxpayer in the country and beyond.

All these different types of information must be protected – they must be kept confidential, so that only authorised people may have access to them; their integrity must be protected, so that only authorised people may change them; and they must be available when required by those who have a need to access them. These three main tenets of information security underpin everything in this book, and are dealt with in greater detail in Chapter 2.

However, in order to protect our own or our organisation's information, we first need to understand exactly what it is and why it is important to the organisation.

An excellent example of the need for protecting information goes back to the 1940s when, during World War II, the British government put up posters declaring 'Careless talk costs lives'. The meaning was clear. People who were aware of military plans might innocently reveal them by indiscreet conversation, and the consequences could be extreme for the military and civilian personnel who were taking part in those actions or whose environment might be affected as a result of them.

The implication on this poster was that any information revealed could unwittingly lead to a compromise of security, but it gave no indication of how sensitive the information might be, the consequences of revealing it or how it should be protected.

This brings us to the issue of information classification, in which each piece of information can be classified for its sensitivity, handling, storage, access or distribution, and ultimately its disposal. The only problem with information classification is that it does not usually reveal the potential value (monetary or otherwise) of the information either to the organisation itself, or to an adversary who might be able to benefit from obtaining it.

Yet another aspect to be considered is information aggregation, in which small pieces of information (some of which might appear completely trivial) are gathered, often from a variety of sources, and pieced together to provide a clearer picture of the whole.

All these elements are brought together in the techniques we use for information risk management, which allows us to clearly identify those information assets that have value to our organisation, determine the impact on the organisation of their unauthorised distribution, alteration or destruction, assess the vulnerabilities exhibited by them, and assess the events that might bring these about and the likelihood of these occurring.

All this provides us with a measure of the level of risk associated with each type or piece of information, from which we can determine the most appropriate response whilst balancing the possible consequences against the cost of treatment.

Some people believe that risk assessments are only necessary in a health and safety situation, but where personal information is concerned there is also a legal obligation to ensure its proper protection. Principle 7 of the Data Protection Act (1998) states that:

> Appropriate technical and organisational measures shall be taken against unauthorised or unlawful processing of personal data and against accidental loss or destruction of, or damage to, personal data.

As already mentioned, information is not restricted to the IT department, so every part of an organisation can benefit from the use of information risk management.

If we are going to protect our information assets, we need to understand what they are, what might threaten their confidentiality, integrity or availability, how they might be vulnerable to such threats or hazards and how likely these are to occur. This, in short, is the key role of information risk management, the essential components of which are discussed later in this chapter.

THE LEGAL FRAMEWORK

Safeguarding information did not present too many problems until computers, especially personal computers, became widespread. It was only with the introduction of the Computer Misuse Act (CMA) in 1990 that people outside government really began to take unauthorised access to information seriously. Since 1990, earlier legislation has been updated to reflect the changes in the accessibility of information, and other legislation, better designed to protect information, has been developed.

The principal instruments of law regarding information risk management are:

- The Data Protection Act 1998, which deals with maintaining the confidentiality and integrity of information, but not its availability.
- The Computer Misuse Act 1990, which deals with the criminal offence of unauthorised access to computer systems and the information contained within them.

- The Police and Criminal Evidence Act 1984, together with subsequent addenda, which deals in part with the proper securing of information-based evidence such as computer files.

- The Official Secrets Act 1989, which deals with the disclosure of nationally sensitive information.

- The Freedom of Information Act 2000, which allows requests to be made regarding rights of access to information held by government organisations.

- The Regulation of Investigatory Powers Act (RIPA) 2000, which deals with information that may be collected by governmental organisations in the pursuit of criminal investigations.

- The Copyright, Designs and Patents Act (CDPA) 1988, which defines copyright as a property right which subsists in the following areas: original literary, dramatic, musical or artistic works; sound recordings, films or broadcasts; and the typographical arrangement of published editions.

All of these relate in one way or another to information risk, and many require that the organisations collecting and holding information must take all reasonable steps to ensure its safety.

Regulation in the information risk management space is less prevalent, although the financial sector does have some regulation regarding risk generally; it is more connected with the management of business risk than information.

Standards and guidelines, however, are available in abundance, and the glossary in this book lists the principle publications in this area.

THE CONTEXT OF RISK IN THE ORGANISATION

Any work on information risk in the organisation must begin with an understanding of the organisation's wider view of business risk, which must necessarily examine the impacts or consequences of unexpected events. These can result in any of the following:

- Financial loss, which can include loss of business or intellectual property.

- Legal and regulatory penalties, which can arise from either a breach of regulatory practice or failing to meet regulatory deadlines.

- Reputational damage, which generally begins with adverse reports in the media.

- Damage to the organisation's operations, which may result in subsequent reputational damage.

- Harm to the organisation's staff or the public-at-large, which again can result from damage to the organisation's operations and reputation.

Although many of these are not based on pure finance, the bottom line is that it is mostly about money, since many of the other types of impact will ultimately result in some form of financial loss, whether directly or indirectly.

Information risk is a subset of business risk and relates to the confidentiality, integrity and availability of business information assets and the information management infrastructure, and although we shall deal with the specific minutiae of impacts to the organisation's information assets, the general principles of business risk management still apply.

Some of the damage to the organisation will be as a result of failures of technology, whilst other damage will be due to failures to follow policies, processes or procedures, and some will be due to events that simply happen.

A wide range of factors affect the organisation's business risk environment, beginning with generic operational disruptions, which affect all organisations, public and private, regardless of sector or size, such as dramatic changes in the economic or political environment, the failure of business transactions that might result from poor management decisions or the failure of parts of the organisation's infrastructure.

Other disruptions that are totally outside the control of any organisation, but which can affect a wide range of organisations, include natural disasters, such as flooding and severe weather, terrorism and civil unrest, all of which will disrupt not only normal business operations, but also those of the public-at-large.

Other types of disruption will come within the control of the organisation, and are often sector-specific, especially in the area of hazardous operational environments such as petrochemicals and energy production. Disruptions from failures in business processes and systems will normally come within the remit of business continuity management, which, although linked to information risk management, is a subject area in its own right.

Organisations in certain sectors will also be subject to the dictates of legal and regulatory bodies, where both generic and sector-specific statutory regulations place additional responsibilities on the organisation. In those organisations where products and services fall within the range of hazardous products, the organisation will be subject to additional societal responsibilities under regulations such as the Control Of Major Accident Hazards (COMAH), and may also be required to cooperate with emergency responders under the Civil Contingencies Act 2004 (CCA) in order to provide protection not only for their staff within the working environment, but also for the general public.

The culture of the organisation itself will have a dramatic effect on business risk. The most visible of these in a business risk context is that of the organisation's risk appetite and the internal awareness the organisation has regarding planning for risk. Whilst they sound similar in nature, risk awareness and risk appetite are quite different – awareness meaning that the organisation recognises risk in all its forms, whereas risk appetite means the level of risk that the organisation will accept in any given situation.

Some organisations maintain an extremely low risk appetite, for example pharmaceutical research organisations take almost no risks at all when it comes to developing a new drug, although it could be said that the potential development costs are a business risk in themselves.

Other organisations thrive on risk – insurance companies and investment brokers being classic examples. This is where risk can be seen as opportunity as opposed to danger.

The reach – local, regional, national, continental or global – of the organisation, together with its business structure and the operational demands it places on its staff, will also be a major contributory factor, and the organisation's hierarchy and reporting channels will define to a great extent the roles and responsibilities of key staff and their accountability for risk.

Very often, those organisations whose operations have a greater degree of urgency will have an increased risk appetite, and may actively encourage staff to take risks within defined limits.

When it comes to information risk, some organisations will maintain extreme secrecy over their entire operations, whilst others will focus more on information that is either sensitive or confidential.

THE BENEFITS OF TAKING ACCOUNT OF INFORMATION RISK

As we have seen from the previous section, risk is inherent in any organisation or business, and failure to take account of risk in any context can be disastrous. This is also true of information risk, in which information that is critical to the survival of the organisation must be protected, or the consequences could be severe and the organisation could be subject to the same types of impact or consequence.

Information risk management – a subset of business risk management – addresses these issues in order to prevent them, and after understanding the business context, organisations will identify risks, analyse, evaluate and treat them.

There are two basic actions that can be used: first, to reduce the likelihood and, second, to reduce the impact or consequence of adverse events. In either case, it is also necessary to limit the possible escalation of events so that matters do not deteriorate once they have begun.

Within the context of information risk management, organisations will need to budget for the prevention of disruptive incidents that would otherwise result in some form of impact and, in those cases where prevention is either not possible or too costly, to budget for the costs of recovery from them.

The potential benefits to organisations of taking serious account of information risk are manifold:

- There will be an improved view within the organisation of the information assets, their value and the degree to which they are protected.
- There will be a noticeable decrease in the overall level of risk borne by the organisation.

- There will almost certainly be a reduction in premiums for those information assets that the organisation insures when transferring or sharing the risk.

- There will be an enhanced view of the organisation in the eyes of its various stakeholders and the media.

- The organisation will be able to respond to, and recover from, disruptive events more quickly and more effectively.

- There will be reduced levels of impact and loss when unexpected events occur.

- The organisation will be able to claim commercial advantage over those of its competitors that do not follow an information risk management strategy.

Information risk management is a 'must' for organisations that are seeking to gain accreditation against ISO/IEC 27001 (Information security management systems) and/or ISO 22301 (Business continuity management systems).

Capability maturity model

For those organisations that decide to invest seriously in information risk management, there is also the option of gaining additional benefit from following the so-called Capability Maturity Model[1], or CMM, which can be used for almost any business function including information risk management.

The CMM consists of five levels of capability maturity:

Level 1 – Initial

Processes at this level are typically undocumented and in a state of dynamic change, tending to be driven in an ad hoc, uncontrolled and reactive manner by users or events.

Level 2 – Repeatable

Processes at this level are repeatable, possibly with consistent results. Process discipline is unlikely to be rigorous, but where it exists it may help to ensure that existing processes are maintained during times of stress.

Level 3 – Defined

Processes at this level are defined and documented standard processes established and subject to some degree of improvement over time. These standard processes are in place and are used to establish consistency of process performance across the organisation.

Level 4 – Managed

Processes at this level use process metrics. Management can effectively control the process and, in particular, can identify ways to adjust and adapt the process to particular projects without measurable losses of quality or deviations from specifications.

Level 5 – Optimising

It is a characteristic of processes at this level that the focus is on continually improving process performance through both incremental and innovative technological changes/improvements.

---

[1] Details of the CMM may be found at http://www.cmmiinstitute.com

ISO/IEC 15504-2 and COBIT 5©

Along similar lines, there is also reference to a measurement framework for process capability in ISO/IEC 15504-2 *Software engineering – Process assessment – Part 2: Performing an assessment*. The identical generic process capability attributes appear in COBIT 5:[2]

Level 0 – Incomplete

The process is not implemented, or fails to achieve its process purpose. At this level there is little or no evidence of any systematic achievement of the process purpose.

Level 1: Performed process

The implemented process achieves its process purpose.

Level 2: Managed process

The previously described Performed process is now implemented in a managed fashion (planned, monitored and adjusted) and its work products are appropriately established, controlled and maintained.

Level 3: Established process

The previously described Managed process is now implemented using a defined process that is capable of achieving its process outcomes.

Level 4: Predictable process

The previously described Established process now operates within defined limits to achieve its process outcomes.

Level 5: Optimising process

The previously described Predictable process is continuously improved to meet relevant current and projected business goals.

OVERVIEW OF THE INFORMATION RISK MANAGEMENT PROCESS

Figure 1.2 illustrates the generic information risk management process, found in a number of standards, including ISO/IEC 27005, ISO/IEC 31000 and ISO/IEC 31010. Whilst being a useful aide memoire, it does suffer from being rather high level, and fails to show the more detailed steps involved. In later chapters of this book, we expand this diagram to explain the steps more fully.

At a very high level, the information risk management process consists of four key steps:

1. The identification and qualification of inherent risk – that is, the risk that an activity would pose if no controls or other mitigating factors were in place.
2. Decision-making regarding the most appropriate form of risk treatment for the risks identified in step 1.

---

[2] Details of the COBIT 5 attributes can be found at http://www.isaca.org/COBIT

3. The application of suitable controls to achieve the objectives determined in step 2.

4. The acceptance of any residual risk following the implementation of the controls applied in step 3.

Naturally, this process only scratches the surface of information risk management, and each of these steps is covered in much greater detail in the remaining chapters of this book.

The process itself begins with gaining an understanding of the context in which the organisation finds itself, and includes both the internal context – that is strategies and policies from within the organisation itself, and the external context, which includes areas such as legal and regulatory constraints, and so on. This is dealt with in greater detail in Chapter 3.

Once the organisational context has been established, the process can continue with the risk assessment, which is broken down into three distinct phases: first, the identification of the risk, this is dealt with in Chapters 4 and 5; second, risk analysis, and finally risk evaluation, which are both dealt with in Chapter 6.

Following this, the process takes us into the realm of risk treatment, which is discussed in Chapter 7, with risk reporting and presentation covered in Chapter 8.

Figure 1.2 The overall risk management process

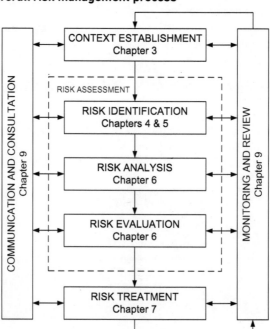

At each stage, there are links between the various steps and those of communication and consultation, in which a dialogue is conducted with major stakeholders, and finally also with the process of monitoring and review, both of which are covered in Chapter 9.

The remaining chapters in this book are organised as follows.

Chapter 2 Review of information security fundamentals

This chapter includes a review of basic information security fundamentals, the process of information classification and the Plan-Do-Check-Act model.

Chapter 3 The information risk management programme

This chapter deals with the goals, scope and objectives, roles and responsibilities, and governance of an information risk management programme, and information risk management criteria.

Chapter 4 Risk identification

In this chapter, we deal with the approach to risk identification, how information assets and their owners are identified, how a business impact analysis is conducted and the types of impact we might encounter, and discusses the pros and cons of qualitative and quantitative assessments.

Chapter 5 Threat and vulnerability assessment

In this chapter, we describe how threat and vulnerability assessments are carried out and also examine the view of existing controls.

Chapter 6 Risk analysis and risk evaluation

In this chapter, we cover the process of assessing the likelihood of risks arising, combining the likelihood with the impacts or consequences of a threat and calculating the relative levels of risk for each threat type.

We then examine how the risk matrix is developed and evaluate the risks in terms of priority.

Chapter 7 Risk treatment

This chapter discusses the approach to making risk treatment plans, and describes the four strategic, four tactical and three operational risk treatment options.

Chapter 8 Risk reporting and presentation

In this chapter, we describe how to report and present the findings of the risk assessment process and explain the need for robust business cases.

Chapter 9 Communication, consultation, monitoring and review

This chapter includes details of the importance of consulting with stakeholders throughout the entire risk management process, and with the process of monitoring and reviewing the work undertaken and how the risk management programme should continue.

Chapter 10 The CESG IA certification scheme

In this chapter, we describe the CESG Certification for Information Assurance Professionals (CCP) scheme, the Skills Framework for the Information Age (SFIA) levels and the IISP skills framework upon which the scheme is largely based.

Chapter 11 HMG security-related documents

This chapter provides a detailed summary of the UK Government (HMG) approach to information risk management, and includes descriptions of the HMG Security Policy Framework, the security of information, and UK Government Security Classifications.

Appendix A Taxonomies and descriptions

In this Appendix, we provide two useful taxonomies that can be used in information risk management: information risk and typical impacts or consequences.

Appendix B Typical threats and hazards

Appendix C Typical vulnerabilities

Appendix D Information risk controls

Appendix E Methodologies, guidelines and tools

In this Appendix, we provide a brief description of some of the more popular information risk management methodologies:

- CORAS;
- CRAMM;
- FAIR;
- IRAM;
- OCTAVE;
- SABSA.

Appendix F Templates

In this Appendix, we provide a number of useful templates and guidance information that can be used in the information risk management programme:

- impact assessment template;
- threat/hazard assessment template;
- vulnerability assessment template;
- existing controls assessment template;
- risk register template.

Appendix G HMG cyber security guidelines

This Appendix discuses the HMG Cyber Essentials Scheme and 10 Steps to Cyber Security.

Appendix H References and further reading

- primary UK legislation;
- good practice guidelines;
- other reference material;
- CESG Certified Professional Scheme;
- other UK Government publications;
- risk management methodologies;
- news articles;
- UK and International standards.

2 REVIEW OF INFORMATION SECURITY FUNDAMENTALS

Having set the scene in terms of definitions, standards and guidelines, the time is right to take a brief look back at the fundamental concepts of information security, as it is these that will form the basis of the risk assessment process itself.

It is a widely held belief that the three main pillars of information security are confidentiality, integrity and availability, often referred to simply as 'CIA'. Whilst this is essentially true, other factors also contribute to the overall scheme of things. Accountability, authenticity, non-repudiation and reliability are all contributing factors, and need to be considered along with the 'main' three.

Let us take a look at some definitions and explanations of these, together with those for information assurance (IA), information governance and data governance.

Confidentiality – the 'property that information is not made available or disclosed to unauthorised individuals, entities or processes' (ISO/IEC 27000:2014). Confidentiality is concerned with ensuring that information is available to authorised entities, and is not allowed to become available to unauthorised entities, whether they are able to do so deliberately or by accident. It follows therefore that users should only have as much access as they require in order to carry out their task and a formal process is required in order to administer access rights.

Privacy and secrecy – both the terms 'private' and 'secret' have the same basic meaning, but, whereas privacy generally indicates the need to protect an individual's information, secrecy can be seen to have a darker side and can indicate a more sinister motive.

Integrity – the 'property of accuracy and completeness' (ISO/IEC 27000:2014). Whilst this definition is fine as far as it goes, the term 'integrity' also suggests a high degree of reliability and assurance, and can apply equally to people as well as to information. Integrity considers both the completeness and accuracy of the information, and, as with confidentiality, users should only have as much access as they require in order to carry out their task and a formal process is required in order to administer access rights.

At best, integrity failures can lead to misinterpretation or poor decision-making; at worst they can lead to serious financial impact and embarrassment to the organisation.

Availability – the 'property of being accessible and usable upon demand by an authorised entity' (ISO/IEC 27000:2014). Availability is often considered the poor relation of CIA, and whilst the other two are very important, if information is not available it becomes frustrating to those who require access to it at the time they require it, and under certain circumstances can have extremely severe consequences.

Availability is now a critical element in the delivery or provision of information; not only to customers who shop online at any hour of the day or night, but also to multinational organisations operating across multiple time zone boundaries.

Also – a business continuity (BC) issue – the tolerable length of time for which any information asset is unavailable may well vary from one organisation to another.

Non-repudiation – the 'ability to prove the occurrence of a claimed event or action and its originating entities' (ISO/IEC 27000:2014). Non-repudiation can be used both to prove not only that an entity has carried out a certain action but also that an entity has not carried out an action, whether this be carrying out a commercial transaction, editing a document or sending an email. An example of non-repudiation is the use of digital signatures and certificates, which are used to establish the identity of an individual beyond all reasonable doubt.

Authentication – the 'provision of assurance that a claimed characteristic of an entity is correct' (ISO/IEC 27000:2014). In order to ensure both confidentiality and integrity, authentication mechanisms are used to validate an entity's credentials – this can be either an individual or an application requiring access to information or applications. Authentication mechanisms include such things as passwords, fingerprint and iris scanning and token generators.

Identification – this is a mechanism by which an entity begins the process of authentication. It may refer to systems, peripherals, people or processes. For example, a user may submit his or her identification in the form of a UserId when logging on to a system or application.

Accountability – 'the assignment of actions and decisions to an entity' (ISO/IEC 27000:2012 – for some reason, the term 'accountability' has been omitted from the ISO/IEC 27000:2014 version). Accountability is often confused with responsibility. The two are very different; an entity may be made responsible for carrying out an action, for example an engineer may be responsible for configuring firewall rules, whereas a more senior manager is likely to be accountable for the firewall and/or its rule-set, and may be held to account if things go wrong.

Accountability is also linked to non-repudiation, in that it may be desirable to correlate transactions with individuals or processes.

Reliability – 'property of consistent intended behaviour and results' (ISO/IEC 27000:2014). Reliability has similar connotations to integrity, but whereas integrity refers mainly to ensuring accuracy and completeness, reliability leans more towards something that can be repeated with accuracy, for example a process that works in a consistent manner every time.

Information assurance – IA is the practice of assuring information and managing risks related to the use, processing, storage and transmission of information or data and the systems and processes used for those purposes.

IA includes protection of the confidentiality, integrity, availability, authenticity and non-repudiation of information. It uses physical, technical and procedural controls to accomplish these tasks.

Whilst focused predominantly on information in digital form, the full range of IA encompasses not only digital information but also analogue or physical information. Protection applies to information in transit, both in physical and electronic forms as well as information at rest in various types of physical and electronic storage facilities. IA as a subject area has grown from the practice of information security.

Information governance – information governance is the set of multi-disciplinary structures, policies, procedures, processes and controls implemented to manage information at an enterprise level, supporting an organisation's immediate and future regulatory, legal, risk, environmental and operational requirements.

Data governance – data governance refers to the general management of key data resources in a company or organisation. This broad term encompasses elements of data use, storage and maintenance, including security issues and the way data flows from one point to another in an overall information technology architecture.

Because data or raw information is a key resource for most businesses and organisations, data governance is a logical area of overall information technology strategy focus for many large enterprises.

INFORMATION CLASSIFICATION

The importance of information classification

All information assets have some degree of value to the organisation. Unless users of these understand their sensitivity and how to deal with them, they could unwittingly – or even deliberately – make them available to unauthorised or unsuitable recipients to the detriment of the organisation or themselves. So, when dealing with either raw data or processed information, whether it is our own or someone else's, it is vital to ensure that users of this understand fully how to access, process, store, transmit, transport and (if necessary) ultimately destroy it. This is otherwise referred to as data or information handling.

To provide these handling specifications for each individual item of data or information would be an enormous task, so, in order to simplify matters, we first classify each data or information item according to a set of rules, which will then allow us to specify the handling procedures for each type.

Within government circles this has been undertaken for many years and is a well-established process. In the private sector, however, although organisational data or information handling guidelines may exist, they are not always rigorously enforced, and in some sectors organisations that do not adequately classify and protect certain types of information may face regulatory penalties. Further, any organisation wishing to attain an accreditation relating to information risk will have to satisfy the accreditor that due diligence has been undertaken, and that information has been classified appropriately.

The term 'privacy marking' is also used in connection with this topic, but differs from information classification in one critical respect – privacy marking deals solely with the labels applied to the information, whereas information classification deals with the privacy marking and the handling of information.

Information classification includes all forms of media, whether in storage (at rest) or in transit from one location to another, such as:

- magnetic media, including hard disks, USB sticks and magnetic tape, locally or in the cloud;
- PDAs, tablet computers, mobile phones and digital cameras;
- optical media, including CDs, DVDs and microfiche;
- paper, including handwritten notes, printed files, diagrams and plans;
- information passing across both wireless and wired networks, including telephone calls, video calls and facsimile transmissions;
- email, text messages and related social media such as Facebook, LinkedIn and Twitter.

Their value of information assets to the organisation or individual is not necessarily limited to their commercial value, but also the impact they could have on the organisation or individuals were they to become known to an attacker, a competitor, a hostile state or the public-at-large.

All information assets must be identified and rated in value against an agreed impact system – a form of risk assessment in itself. The UK Government has recently (April 2014) published an updated information classification scheme, which greatly simplifies the previous system:

- Top secret – HMG's most sensitive information requiring the highest levels of protection from the most serious threats. For example, where compromise could cause widespread loss of life or else threaten the security or economic wellbeing of the country or friendly nations.
- Secret – very sensitive information that justifies heightened protective measures to defend against determined and highly capable threat actors. For example, where compromise could seriously damage military capabilities, international relations or the investigation of serious organised crime.
- Official – the majority of information that is created or processed by the public sector. This includes routine business operations and services, some of which could have damaging consequences if lost, stolen or published in the media, but are not subject to a heightened threat profile.

Commercial organisations, on the other hand, may have a system such as:

- Strictly confidential – the loss or damage of which could cause extremely serious financial impact or embarrassment to the organisation. This might include future business plans, future product development information or information that might have an adverse effect on the organisation's share value.

- Confidential – the loss or damage of which could cause some financial impact or embarrassment to the organisation.

- Personal – the loss or damage of which could cause some financial impact or embarrassment to one or more individuals within the organisation, and could have regulatory repercussions on the organisation.

- Internal use only – the impact of which might be low, but could be aggregated with other information for use by a competitor.

- Public – which can be made available to any person or organisation.

In order to assign privacy markings, the concepts of confidentiality, integrity and availability must be taken into account. For example, any information asset labelled as strictly confidential would almost certainly have a very high degree of all three, whereas public information need only have a certain degree of integrity and availability.

In terms of confidentiality, the most frequently used guideline is referred to as the 'need-to-know' principle – information should not be made available to people who do not need to know it. Integrity is often addressed by segregation or separation of duties, so that one person might generate information, but in order for it to be made available it may need to be verified by a second person. Availability is most frequently addressed by the use of backups, DR and BC plans, processes and procedures.

In addition to these privacy markings, information can also be assigned caveats, known in government circles as descriptors. These are additional attributes that ensure a finer layer of granularity. Some examples are:

- HR only – referring to personnel files containing sensitive personal data.

- XXX Project Team only – not to be shown to anyone who is not a member of a particular project team.

- Not for general release until xxx – not to be further distributed until a certain date.

Another information classification scheme has become popular in recent years, which emanates from the UK's Centre for the Protection of National Infrastructure (CPNI), known as the 'Traffic Light Protocol' (TLP). This uses a simple colour code to identify the sensitivity of information.

The general definitions are as follows:

- RED – Personal for Named Recipients Only – in the context of a meeting, for example, distribution of RED information is limited to those present at the meeting, and in most circumstances will be passed verbally or in person.

- AMBER – Limited Distribution – recipients may share AMBER information with others within their organisation, but only on a 'need-to-know' basis. The originator may be expected to specify the intended limits of that sharing.

- GREEN – Community-wide – information in this category can be circulated widely within a particular community or organisation. However, the information may not be published or posted on the Internet, nor released outside of the community.

- WHITE – Unlimited – subject to standard copyright rules, WHITE information may be distributed freely and without restriction.

Once information assets have been identified, it will be necessary to match each of them (or groups of similar information assets) against an information owner. There must then be a process in which the security classification of the information assets are verified through interviews with the information owners.

Handling of information assets

Once the security classification scheme has been established, thought must be given to how the information asset is handled.

Creation and storage of an information asset

The originator or creator of any information asset should consider assigning its security classification immediately, especially if the information is of a sensitive nature. Even if the information asset is in draft form – for example, an early version of a project plan, design or simple document – it should be stored in the most appropriate manner.

Not only can the item be stored in a secure location, but it might also be necessary to password protect the item as an additional means of securing it, or by encrypting the item when stored.

Sharing and review of an information asset

Once an information asset has been created, it is possible that other people will review it; for example, a draft project plan might require input from a number of team members, each of whom may need to view and update the plan. This brings in another level of protection – that of the item's security attributes, and the ability of individuals to read from and write to the item.

If multiple people are able to access the item simultaneously, there needs to be a 'lockout' mechanism to prevent more than one person trying to edit the item at the same time.

For this reason, and in order to minimise the possibility of an item going astray, sharing is better achieved by allowing controlled, shared access to it, rather than by sending it by email for example.

Transmission of an information asset

At times, it will be necessary to transmit the information to another person, and the security of the information during transit must be considered. Depending upon the sensitivity of the information, it may be possible to transmit it over a public network such as the Internet, a virtual private network (VPN) or a heavily secured private network such as the Government Secure Intranet (GSI); some information may be required to be encrypted when transmitted, or it may have to be hand carried by courier in a highly secure briefcase.

Disposal of an information asset

Most information assets will have some kind of life expectancy, and once this point in time has been reached, it may be necessary or desirable to dispose of the asset rather than storing it indefinitely. Suitable methods of destruction will depend as always on the sensitivity of the information, and may range from simple file deletion for an unclassified asset to physical destruction of the platters of a hard disk drive or from shredding to burning of paper documents.

The main point for any system of information classification is that, once an information asset has been given a security classification, it automatically imposes constraints on the methods that can be used to process, store, transmit and ultimately dispose of it. These conditions must inevitably be imposed on anyone who may come into contact with that information asset.

Because the nature and sensitivity of information assets may change over time, a periodic review of information assets and their classifications is essential.

PLAN, DO, CHECK, ACT

Although it is not, strictly speaking, an information risk topic, for many years, and for a variety of purposes, organisations have made use of a system known as the Plan-Do-Check-Act (PDCA) cycle, illustrated in Figure 2.1.

Figure 2.1 The Plan-Do-Check-Act cycle

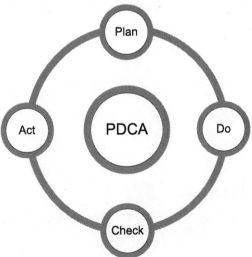

The PDCA cycle has been widely adopted as a basic reference framework in information security, information risk management and BC management disciplines as well as many others.

The four stages are:

- PLAN

  In this stage, we establish the objectives and the processes necessary to deliver the required results. In the information risk management context, this equates to understanding the organisation and its context.

- DO

  The next stage of the process implements the plan, initially as a means of testing that the plan has been successful. In the information risk management context, this equates to implementation of the information risk management framework.

- CHECK

  In this stage, we examine the results we have achieved either by measurement or by observation. In the information risk management context, this equates to monitoring and review of the framework.

- ACT

  In the final stage, we put the validated plans into action when an incident occurs and bring lessons learnt from incidents into revision of the plan. In the information risk management context, this equates to continual improvement of the framework.

Earlier British and international standards made considerable use of this in their introductory sections, but, since 2013, use of the PDCA cycle has diminished.

3 THE INFORMATION RISK MANAGEMENT PROGRAMME

Due to its possible scale, for many organisations risk management will involve a programme of work rather than simply a project, and whilst the mechanics of managing information risk are relatively straightforward, there needs to be an overall framework around the activity if there is to be any real chance of success.

The organisation should ideally establish an information risk management programme, which will have oversight of the work. Such a programme might contain the following elements:

- The goals, scope and objectives of the programme and the organisation's overall information risk management policy.
- The overall roles and responsibilities of the programme leaders and key players, including their authorities, ownership and accountability.
- The governance processes for the programme and, if necessary, those for the individual components within the programme.
- The internal standards that must be observed, including risk criteria, reporting, documentation and management processes.
- The financial arrangements including budget if these are known.
- Training of those involved in the programme and awareness for staff generally.
- Monitoring and review of progress and results.

Many organisations make use of the PDCA model, described in greater detail in Chapter 2. PDCA is a useful method in the management of any project or programme, but although it has featured in many UK and international standards, more recently published standards have omitted it.

The PDCA model takes the view that although an information risk management programme may have defined start and finish points, it is in fact a continuous process, and that organisation should revisit all risks on a regular basis or when any facet changes. This highlights the need for the integration of information risk management into business-as-usual operations.

GOALS, SCOPE AND OBJECTIVES

The organisation's ultimate goal might be to obtain ISO/IEC 27001 accreditation, and an effective information risk management programme will be an essential component of this.

Alternatively, it may just be the case that the organisation wishes to establish as risk-free an information environment as possible. If the former, the accreditor will be seeking evidence not only of the outcomes of such a programme, but also the means by which it has been executed and its ongoing monitoring. If the latter, it may still be worthwhile the organisation employing the services of an auditor or accreditor simply to verify that the programme has been conducted thoroughly and completely.

In developing the strategic approach to the information risk management programme, the team will be required to establish both the internal and external contexts in which the organisation operates and how the information risk management process fits in to the overall business environment.

A key aspect of this is the requirement to define, document and agree with senior management the organisation's risk appetite and its criteria for accepting risks that cannot be treated by other means as well as for accepting residual risk.

Many of the drivers for the information risk management programme will originate from the organisation's existing information security policies, and many of the controls applied in order to treat the risks identified will involve information security team involvement.

It is crucial therefore that the information risk management programme is not viewed as being a stand-alone or separate programme from that of the information security community, and that constant communication and consultation takes place between the two disciplines wherever their management structure differs.

Some of the requirement identified by the information risk management programme will originate from the organisation's legal and regulatory requirements, and therefore the legal and regulatory department will be heavily involved, and there will likewise be the need to ensure communications and consultation between stakeholders at all levels, both within the organisation, and outside it where necessary.

Setting the programme scope

Whilst the strategy of the information risk management programme sets out the goals and objectives of the programme, it is also essential to go down a level and set the scope.

This would include those elements of the organisation's information assets that are to be within the scope of the programme and, equally importantly, those elements of the organisation's information assets that are to remain outside the scope of the programme

ROLES AND RESPONSIBILITIES

No programme can be successful unless it has strong leadership, and in setting the overall roles and responsibilities for the programme, the organisation's senior management team must bear in mind that, in addition to leaders, the programme requires dedicated assignment of resources to undertake the detailed work.

Managers of these staff must be made aware of the programme and understand that people will need to take time from other duties in order to take part in the programme, in which they might report to another manager, and that the staff themselves may require additional training.

GOVERNANCE OF THE RISK MANAGEMENT PROGRAMME

Within the overall framework of governance of risk management, there will be three distinct layers of involvement. At the strategic layer, there will be the accountabilities and authorities for the programme, some of which will lie at board level. The designated board member or members should ensure that the tactical and operational work is understood and that the organisation's business and cultural contexts are taken into account.

Legal and regulatory compliance issues can become a complex subject in their own right, especially in cases where organisations are spread across multiple legal and regulatory jurisdictions. The organisation's legal and regulatory department must identify all necessary obligations to the programme, and ensure that these are complied with. However, it will also be necessary to maintain oversight of the legal and regulatory liabilities that exist, since the costs of achieving these may have an impact on the costs of the programme.

In parallel with the identification of any work packages, the nomination of key individuals having specific roles within the programme will have a profound effect on its outcome, and the board will need to ensure that these individuals' performance is monitored and reviewed, and that their terms of reference are verified at intervals to ensure that the programme's objectives are being achieved.

The board should ideally have the information risk management programme as a running agenda item, as it may well be a component part of the organisation's annual reporting, especially if it is in a highly regulated sector.

At the tactical layer, a slightly lower-level view is required, and the adoption of risk intelligence procedures enable the organisation to discover the existence of risks that have either not yet been taken into account – these might be obtained from both business and information security sources – or those that have occurred previously within the organisation. In some contexts, and especially in terms of business continuity, this is known as horizon scanning.

Also within the tactical layer of governance is risk policy management in which a strategic steer from board level is translated into the day-to-day policies that must be followed by the organisation. This includes an overall policy framework and the general format of the policies, together with their interdependencies where these exist.

Finally, at the operational layer, there will be the key activities of the information risk management programme: those of risk assessment, including the identification of threats, vulnerabilities and impacts or consequences; the formulation of the likelihood and subsequent analysis of the risks; and, finally, the evaluation of risks and the proposals for risk treatment.

A final element of the overall programme governance will be the need for regular communications and reporting both upwards and downwards through the chain of command, especially in the reporting and logging of new risks and in the progress in treatment of existing risks.

INFORMATION RISK MANAGEMENT CRITERIA

Internal standards and criteria

In support of the information risk management programme, and to guide its internal standards, there will be a number of business RMR that will be needed.

The legal and regulatory framework in which the organisation operates, both with its host country and other jurisdictions will have a major impact on the standards and criteria adopted. These will include so-called 'primary legislation', the laws of the country concerned, such as the CMA and the DPA, and secondary regulation, which is generally sector-specific.

The nature of business within the sector itself will have some influence on standards and criteria, as well as the way in which the organisation is structured, both organisationally and geographically.

High-level business risk estimation

In order to provide a starting point for the later risk assessment work, the organisation may benefit from producing a series of high-level estimates of business risk. These need not be very specific or accurate, since they are intended only as a 'starter for ten', but might include such areas as the possible losses that might be incurred by the business through being unable to answer customer calls or by being unable to reach a minimum regulatory threshold for some reason.

Important at this stage is the 'what', rather than the 'why', since it will lead the later stages of the work into a more detailed impact analysis and provide the analysts with a number of high-level headings with which to begin their work.

Risk appetite

In order to proceed with the process of information risk management, the organisation must commence by setting its risk appetite. Unfortunately, this is not a one-off exercise, as each type or class of information asset may have a different risk appetite associated with it.

The following factors will determine the risk appetite for each type or class of information:

- the information's classification;
- the information's confidentiality, integrity and availability requirements;

- the organisation's sector type;
- the organisation's culture;
- the organisation's legal and regulatory obligations.

We will deal with impact and likelihood scales in greater detail in Chapter 4, but in the meantime, it is worthwhile understanding that the terms 'low', 'medium' and 'high' are qualitative as they stand and are therefore relatively meaningless – and thus should be placed in a quantitative context. So, for example, 'low' might refer to a range of values up to £100,000; 'medium' to a range between £100,000 and £1 million, and 'high' to a range of values greater than £1 million.

This still does not dictate the exact risk appetite, but it does provide the assessor with reasonable objective guidelines as opposed to less useful subjective ones. Naturally, the level of granularity of the ranges can be increased if desired, but as the level of granularity increases, this brings about a more complex assessment process.

Risk treatment criteria

At the strategic level of risk treatment, there are four basic options:

- risk avoidance or termination;
- risk reduction or modification;
- risk transfer or sharing;
- risk acceptance or tolerance.

Below this are the tactical and operational levels of risk treatment, which we will deal with in greater detail in Chapter 7, but for the moment, we will examine these four in a little greater depth.

There are also several key factors that influence the decision as to which course of action is most appropriate:

- Whether the choice is actually achievable. For example, it may not be possible to take out an insurance policy against the prospect of a fine for violating data protection law.
- Whether the choice brings about additional risk. For example, if the organisation decides not to enter into a new development programme, there may be consequential losses incurred by not doing so.
- Whether multiple choices are appropriate. For example, treating a particular risk might involve halting one part of a business operation, insuring against a capital loss and introducing additional procedures to reduce the likelihood.

Whatever the choice made, it should be understood that there may always be some residual risk, regardless of the effectiveness of the actions taken, and this residual risk will have to be accepted by the organisation, recorded as such and subjected to ongoing monitoring and review. Further, the process for recommending the choice or choices should be according to defined criteria, and should follow a consultative process to ensure both consistency and fairness.

Risk avoidance or termination criteria

These can be quite difficult to define, partly due to the subjective nature of some of the inputs to the decision-making process. Trying to overcome this subjectivity can be a time consuming and expensive process in its own right. For example, if an organisation wishes to undertake a particular activity, but does not feel it possesses the skills and expertise to do so, it may be possible to outsource the work to another organisation. However, without a detailed financial analysis, it might not be clear as to whether the cost of this approach would be greater or less than the losses incurred by not undertaking the activity at all.

Alternatively, the organisation may feel that the risk is so high that the possible costs of treatment would be unacceptable. Again, without further detailed financial analysis, the decision to avoid the risk becomes subjective and subject to a large degree of uncertainty.

The only objective factor driving the decision to avoid or terminate a risk is when the organisation is fully aware without further analysis that the costs of treating the risk exceed the possible impact of not treating it.

Taking the route of risk avoidance will normally remove both the impact and the likelihood of the risk, but may result in some form of consequential risk caused by not undertaking the activity.

Risk reduction or modification criteria

This option allows us to reduce either the impact or the likelihood of the risk, and possibly even both. However, risk reduction does not imply that the risk is reduced to an acceptable level (as determined by the organisation's risk appetite), but merely that it has been reduced to some degree. As mentioned under risk treatment criteria, it may be necessary to use several different forms of risk reduction, or use them in combination with other types of risk treatment.

The decision to reduce or modify a risk will be based on whether or not the costs of doing so are above or below the level set by the organisation's risk appetite for the particular information asset and whether the organisation possesses the skills and expertise to do so from within.

Risk transfer or sharing criteria

In contrast to risk reduction, risk transfer can only ever reduce the impact of a risk, but never the likelihood. In transferring the risk to a third party, the organisation can only transfer the treatment of the risk – the ownership must remain with the organisation. A good example of this is the case of the BP Deepwater Horizon oil spill in 2010, in which almost 5 million barrels of crude oil were discharged into the Gulf of Mexico with disastrous results to the ecology of the region. Although the oilrig was operated by a third-party organisation, the US government held BP responsible for the incident.

Transferring a risk can usually mean insuring against it, but can also refer to outsourcing arrangements, especially of information technology hardware and software and also of information security management.

Transferring risk will have up-front costs (premiums in the case of insurance), and may also have downstream costs; for example, there may be an excess penalty to pay in the event of a claim, and also the policy payment may not fully cover the cost of replacement, repair or recovery if certain exclusions apply through circumstances in force when the risk event takes place.

Finally, transferring the risk depends both upon the availability or willingness of a third party willing to take on the risk, since some risks are not insurable, and the usual constraint of whether the potential losses exceed the potential costs.

Risk acceptance or tolerance criteria

The final choice for risk treatment is that of accepting or tolerating the risk. This must always be done knowingly and objectively, and the residual risk must always be monitored in case either the impact or the likelihood changes with time. Ignoring a risk is never an option since, although it may be very low at one point in time, either the possible impact or the likelihood could increase dramatically or gradually, with the result that it becomes necessary to take an alternative approach to treat the risk.

Accepting risks does not alter either the impact or the likelihood of the risk occurring, and will generally be the option when the costs of treating the risk are greater than the potential losses that might be incurred.

Costs of risk treatment

In a later stage of the information risk management programme, a list of recommendations will be presented to senior management for their consideration before risk treatment commences. Some of these recommendations will require significant financial investment in order to fully treat the risks identified.

For example, the risk of a key system becoming unavailable might be so high that a decision is made to treat it by providing a high-availability standby system.

The magnitude of cost incurred by a project such as this would be very significant, and therefore the organisation's senior management might well request that a full business case be provided, and that a financial threshold is set as an additional criterion for the information risk management programme.

Training

In organisations that are highly developed in terms of capability, the level of training required by staff in the process of information risk management may not be great. However, in those organisations that are less experienced in this kind of work, training of staff at all levels – strategic, tactical and operational – may be a necessary preliminary to the programme.

Many skills are relatively easily learnt, and can be acquired on readily available industry training courses. Others, however, especially in the legal and regulatory domain, may not be so straightforward to acquire, and will need time to develop and possibly considerable mentoring before staff are fully proficient.

The main point of course is that the overall information risk management programme must necessarily include an element of training and development in order to ensure its success.

Communication and consultation

From the very beginning, the information risk management programme will require a high degree of communication up and down the organisation, and the need for consultation, particularly in the early stages of the programme, cannot be overstated.

It is a common mistake for inexperienced information risk managers to make broad assumptions regarding the value of assets, the impacts on the organisation of the loss or damage to those assets, the threats and hazards faced by the assets and the vulnerabilities they exhibit.

The information risk manager should strive to consult at every stage of the programme, and resist the temptation to make rash assumptions, the consequences of which can be highly detrimental.

At an early stage in the programme, the information risk manager should take great care to identify all those who are directly responsible for the information assets in question, or who are able to take an objective view of impacts and consequences, threats or hazards and vulnerabilities, and to make contact with them as soon as possible.

Another common error is to assume that these 'subject matter experts' will either be aware of the programme, its importance to the organisation or the likely involvement they may have in it. Whilst it might be acceptable to fire off a quick 'heads up' email to someone whom the information risk manager knows well, but might be less appropriate for others, it is strongly recommended that contact should be established on a personal level before making regular use of email to exchange information.

Monitoring and review

The final piece in the overall information risk management programme puzzle is that of monitoring and regular review of the entire activity.

It may be useful for the organisation to define some basic metrics for the purpose of monitoring progress. However, care should be taken in being too general in this approach, since the risk management for some risks will take quite a short time, whilst that for others may take significantly longer. It is perhaps better to report on individual areas in terms of percentage completeness, and then to combine these individual amounts to provide an overall status.

Whichever approach is taken, it should be clearly defined and consistently applied, so that different teams report their own activities in the same way as all others, and that the senior management team do not receive a skewed view of overall progress.

Occasionally, risks will emerge that, despite the best efforts of the risk management team, appear to have reached an impasse and that no clear indication can be made as to how – or whether – to treat them. Risks such as these should be flagged to the organisation's senior management team at the earliest possible moment in order to ensure that they do not become overlooked simply because they are too difficult to deal with.

The overall owner and person accountable for the information risk management programme should monitor its progress on a frequent and regular basis, and should make a point of reviewing all risks addressed by the programme whether they have been treated or not, and establish that their treatment is on track.

4 RISK IDENTIFICATION

The first stage of the risk assessment process is that of risk identification, the purpose of which is to determine the threats and hazards that could cause loss or damage to an information asset, to identify any vulnerabilities exhibited by the information asset and to determine the possible impact or consequences to the information asset.

Regardless of whether or not the risks identified fall within the remit of the organisation, they must be included in the assessment, even though the root cause may remain hidden.

Just to recap, an impact on an information asset is the result of a threat or hazard taking advantage of a vulnerability; the likelihood of the threat or hazard succeeding in this depends on the type of threat and any vulnerabilities exhibited by the information asset. Risk is the combination of the impact on the information asset combined with the likelihood of the threat or hazard successfully taking place.

Looking slightly deeper into this, we should also take into account the motivation for the attack for certain types of threat – where an attacker either wishes to obtain or change information (confidentiality or integrity), or to deny access to information asset (availability).

In Figure 4.1, we can see that risk is the result of combining impact and likelihood. The impact is determined by a threat exploiting a vulnerability within an information asset, and that the presence of both threat and vulnerability give rise to the likelihood.

Figure 4.1 A general view of the risk environment

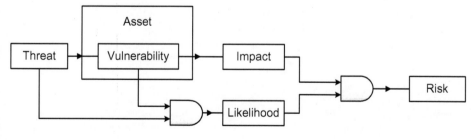

Now let us take a quick look at the more detailed process of risk identification.

Risk identification begins with identifying the information assets that are relevant to the organisation. This is almost certainly the most crucial part of the whole process – failing to identify an asset at this stage will mean it is never risk assessed; and it is vital that, along with the asset itself, an asset owner is identified. For some assets, this will be immediately obvious, whereas for others a senior management decision may be required in order to allocate ownership of the information asset to a suitable person or team.

Once the information assets have been identified, the asset owners can identify the impact or consequences of their damage, loss or destruction. This part of risk identification is commonly referred to as impact assessment.

Let us take a look first at the types of information we might identify. Mostly, these days, we think of information being in electronic form, but it is important to remember other information that remains in the form of paper documents, microfiche, microfilm and so on. Also, whilst much of the information we are concerned with will be alphanumeric in nature, there may be other types that are critical to the organisation, such as software, audio and video files, photographs or 'raw' data, such as that recorded from seismographic surveys and weather observations. Figure 4.2 illustrates many types of information, but individual organisations will doubtless identify others that are peculiar to their sector or business type, and which must also be considered.

Figure 4.2 Typical types of information asset

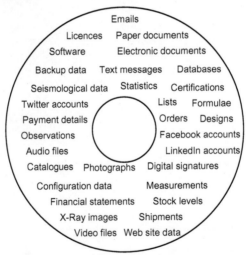

The main factor that will help to identify those information assets that must be within the scope of the programme is a list of business-critical activities. However, even though this will identify many of the organisation's information assets, the business-critical activities themselves should be subjected to some form of analysis to take into account other non-critical activities upon which the business-critical activities have a greater or lesser degree of dependence.

For most organisations, the main areas of information assets may include:

- operational information that underpins the very nature of the organisation, such as customer order history, stock control or product designs;
- personal information as defined within the DPA, such as names, postal and email addresses and telephone numbers;
- strategic information, such as sales forecasts, development schedules or product launch plans;
- information that is expensive to collect, store or process, such as census information.

It is unlikely that information that falls outside these categories will be critical to an organisation's performance, and it may be omitted from the information identification scope with the agreement of the relevant information owners.

THE APPROACH TO RISK IDENTIFICATION

There are several different skills required in order to conduct a successful impact assessment. These are described in greater detail in Chapter 9.

It may be the case that no individual within the organisation possesses all these, in which case the combined skills of two (or possibly more) people may be employed. In any event, it is always advantageous to have a second opinion when undertaking this kind of activity, and another pair of eyes and ears can pick up things that an individual might overlook.

An effective method for commencing an impact assessment is to hold an introductory workshop to inform and engage the senior management team who will then be best positioned to brief their departmental managers and staff on what to expect and what to research. Beyond that, the approach taken for interviews will need to be tailored to the type of audience.

Some interviews are best conducted on a one-to-one basis, especially if there are sensitive issues at stake, whereas others may benefit from a group discussion or workshop in order to ensure that the views of different sections within a department are considered.

Telephone interviews should be avoided where possible unless there is no alternative, as the visual signals given in face-to-face meetings can provide additional clues. Follow-up telephone discussions when reviewing the findings present less of a problem.

At all times, the interviewer should give the interviewee time to reflect on the question, and once an answer has been recorded it is worth the interviewer summarising the discussion as a quick means of verifying the findings. It is also important to choose the order of questions carefully. Questioning should follow a logical sequence – for example, the same sequence as a development or production process in which information is used and generated – in order to permit the interviewee to follow a more logical thought process when answering.

At the beginning of the risk identification process, the most appropriate format of the impact analysis should be agreed with the programme sponsor, although flexibility is always important, and it may be necessary to modify the format as the interviews progress and findings are recorded.

Events or incidents?

For the purposes of this book, we shall refer to events and incidents as having the same characteristics, since both terms are frequently used interchangeably to discuss something detrimental that has occurred. However, it is worth taking a very brief look at how the incident management – especially the BC management – communities view the terms. A general view is illustrated in Table 4.1.

Table 4.1 The general properties of detrimental situations

Seconds	Minutes	Hours	Days	Weeks	Months
Glitch	Event	Incident	Crisis	Disaster	Catastrophe
Equipment		Operations	Management	Board	Government
Automatic		Process	Improvisation	Ad hoc	Rebuild
Proactive			Reactive		

Glitches

Extremely short occurrences are often referred to as glitches. They usually last a few seconds at the most and generally refer to brief interruptions in power, computer processing, television and radio transmissions. Activities usually return to normal following most glitches as equipment self-corrects automatically.

Events

Events normally last no more than a few minutes. Like glitches, the equipment they affect is frequently automatically self-correcting, but may on occasion require a degree of manual intervention.

Incidents

Incidents are viewed as lasting no more than a few hours. Unlike glitches and events, they require operational resolution, normally requiring manual intervention that follows some form of process.

The methods of dealing with glitches, events and incidents are all proactive in nature.

Crises

Crises generally last for several days. Although organisations may have plans, processes and procedures to deal with them, and, although operational staff will carry out any remedial actions, some degree of improvisation may be required. Crises almost invariably require a higher layer of management to take control of the situation, make decisions and communicate with senior management and the media.

Disasters

Disasters generally last for weeks. As with crises, operational staff will carry out remedial actions, although at this stage, a degree of ad hoc action may be necessary and although a higher management layer will control activities, the senior management layer will take overall charge of the situation.

Catastrophes

Catastrophes are the most serious level, often lasting for months or, in some cases, for years. Their scale tends to affect many communities and so, although individual organisations may be operating their own recovery plans, it is likely that local, regional or even national government will oversee the situation and that a complete rebuilding of the infrastructure may be required.

Despite any proactive planning or activities to lessen their impact or likelihood, crises, disasters and catastrophes all require reactive activities.

Incidents, crises, disasters and catastrophes generally follow a set sequence of planning, preparation and testing, incident response, BC operations and resumption to normal operations, as shown in Figure 4.3.

Figure 4.3 Generic sequence of situation management

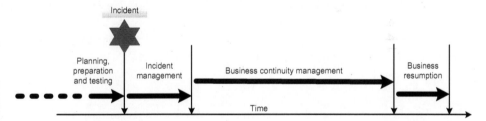

IMPACT ASSESSMENT

The next real piece of work in risk assessment is that of identifying the impacts or consequences to the information assets.

Let us begin by understanding what actually comprises impact or consequence. In general terms, an impact is the adverse result of some action (a threat or hazard), taking advantage of a weakness or vulnerability in an information asset, as shown in Figure 4.4.

Figure 4.4 A simple threat, vulnerability and impact

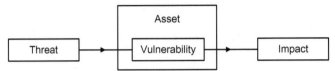

However, the situation is not always as simple as this, since there can be more than one threat against an information asset that takes advantage of the same vulnerability and results in the same impact, as shown in Figure 4.5.

Figure 4.5 Multiple threats can exploit the same vulnerability

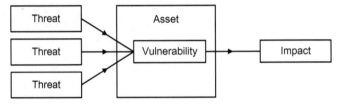

Also, of course, it is quite possible that an information asset exhibits a number of vulnerabilities, and that a single threat attacks each, resulting in a number of different impacts, depicted in Figure 4.6.

Figure 4.6 A single threat can exploit multiple vulnerabilities

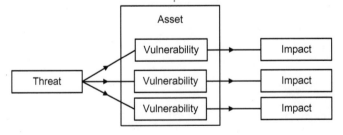

Finally, there is the so-called 'knock-on effect' or 'chain of consequence', in which a threat exploits a vulnerability in one information asset and the resulting impact becomes a threat to another information asset, and so on. These chains of consequence can be quite complicated to follow, but whenever impact assessments are carried out, it should be borne in mind that such a chain may well exist, and where the assessor can imagine links of dependencies between information assets, the possibility of such a chain should be consciously explored.

Figure 4.7 illustrates a chain of consequence. A threat exploits a vulnerability in asset 1, resulting in an impact that has a knock-on effect to become the threat facing assets 2 and 3, and in turn the impact on asset 3 becomes the threat that affects asset 4.

An excellent example of chains of consequence would be the failure in a fully automated environment of an organisation's order processing system. Without the output from this, the organisation's production line would not be able to produce the order, the despatch department would have nothing to deliver and the billing department would be unable to produce an invoice.

Figure 4.7 A typical chain of consequence

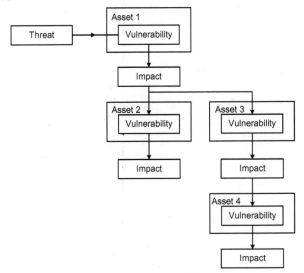

When examining chains of consequence, it is important that progress through the chain is traced back to its root cause – sometimes referred to as 'root cause analysis', since it is the root cause that triggers all the subsequent impacts.

TYPES OF IMPACT

Before we examine the various types of impact, we need to understand that they will affect the organisation in slightly different ways, depending on their origin. On the first level, there are two categories:

Primary or **immediate** impacts result from the event itself, when a business function is detrimentally affected or unable to continue. They have two sub-categories:

- Direct primary impacts. For example, if a customer database is hacked and personal information is stolen, the organisation will lose control of that valuable information resource.

41

- Indirect primary impacts. Indirect impacts may occur as a consequence of the direct impact. As an example, the Information Commissioner may levy a fine against the organisation for failing to adequately protect the information.

Secondary or **future** impacts are those that result from responding to or recovering from the event. Again, there are two categories:

- Direct secondary impacts include such things as customers purchasing their products or services from another supplier.

- Indirect secondary impacts include such things as fines imposed for failing to file statutory returns on time because the necessary information is unavailable.

Figure 4.8 takes the 'simple' impact model described above, and breaks it down further:

Figure 4.8 Impact types

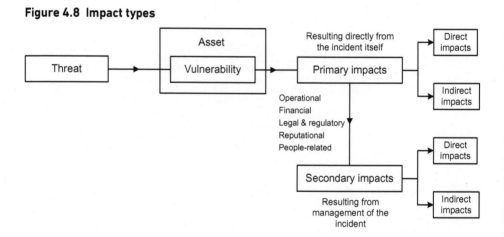

For the purposes of this book, we have organised impacts into five types, and we shall examine each in greater detail:

- operational impacts;
- financial impacts;
- legal and regulatory impacts;
- reputational impacts;
- impacts on the wellbeing of staff and the public-at-large.

Operational impacts

As the name suggests, operational impacts impair the day-to-day activities of the organisation. Very often, direct operational impacts will result in subsequent indirect financial impacts, so an inability to meet a service contract may well result in lost orders or claims for contractual damages. These include (but are not limited to):

- the loss of or damage to the confidentiality, integrity or availability of information;
- the loss of or damage to premises and equipment;
- order backlogs;
- productivity losses;
- industrial action;
- reduced competitive capability;
- the organisation's inability to meet service contracts;
- the organisation's inability to progress new business or developments;
- damage to third-party relations;
- impaired management control;
- the loss of customers to competitors, known in some sectors as 'churn'.

Most operational impacts are felt by the organisation very quickly – their presence will usually be very obvious, and not only within the organisation itself, but also to the public-at-large and the media. Because of this, operational impacts are frequently dealt with in a reactive way by invoking some form of incident management process to bring the situation under control, recover from the incident and eventually return to normal. Incident management is more usually associated with business continuity, but very much has a place in information risk management as well.

Financial impacts

Unsurprisingly, financial impacts or consequences are normally those that gain the greatest attention within the organisation. It is frequently against a backdrop of possible financial loss that the costs of remedial actions will be compared. Whilst this is certainly correct, it is also true for other types of impact as well:

- loss of current and future business opportunities;
- increased cost of borrowing;
- cancellation of contracts;
- contractual penalties;
- loss of cash flow;
- replacement and redevelopment costs;
- loss of share price;
- increased insurance premiums;
- loss of tangible assets.

Many of these impacts – for example, lost sales immediately following the event – will be felt very quickly, whilst others – for example, increased insurance premiums – may not manifest themselves until a later date, possibly some time after the costs of the event have been counted.

Financial impacts may also not be as noticeable to the whole organisation – for example, staff may not be aware of the financial implications of an event at all, and have no appreciation of the position in which the organisation finds itself until they read about it in the media or find that pay increases and bonuses are reduced.

Legal and regulatory impacts

As with reputational impacts, legal and regulatory impacts can have serious repercussions on an organisation, and the handling of these is best dealt with by a specialist team within the organisation, who may communicate information regarding an event through the corporate communication department. Legal and regulatory impacts, which can also be referred to as consequential losses, include:

- warnings or penalties from sector regulator;
- fines for late submission of company accounts;
- fines for late payment of taxes;
- breach of contract damages;
- fraud and other criminal acts.

Reputational impacts

Reputational impacts are almost always highly detrimental to the organisation. For this reason, many organisations employ communication specialists who are skilled in countering negative publicity and putting a positive spin on any bad news. In such organisations, most staff are advised not to talk directly to the media, but to pass enquiries through to the corporate communication department. Reputational impacts, which can also be referred to as consequential losses, include:

- stock market confidence;
- competitors taking advantage;
- customer perception;
- public perception;
- industry and institutional image;
- confidential information made public.

The reputation of an organisation can be destroyed overnight. Take the case of the Gerald Ratner chain of cut-price jewellery shops in the 1990s. Ratner made a speech at the Institute of Directors during which he made several derogatory remarks about the products he sold. Despite the fact that he had thought the remarks were 'off the cuff', they were reported in the press and customers exacted their revenge by staying away. The value of the organisation plummeted by around £500 million, and the company very nearly ceased trading.

Wellbeing of staff and the public-at-large

Although more rare, safety incidents are generally highly visible outside the organisation, and occasionally have an impact on the public-at-large. More common, however, are any events that may have an adverse effect on the organisation's staff, and these can also cascade into financial and operational secondary impacts. Wellbeing impacts include:

- safety, health risks and injuries;
- stress and trauma;
- low morale of staff.

QUALITATIVE AND QUANTITATIVE ASSESSMENTS

Qualitative assessments are almost always subjective. The terms 'low', 'medium' and 'high' give a general indication of the level of impact, but do not tell us how much. Quantitative assessments, on the other hand, can be very specific, and rather more accurate. The main problem with quantitative assessments is that, if they are to be entirely accurate, they can take a great deal of time to undertake and, mostly, total accuracy is not a requirement.

In the case of impact assessment, it may be worthwhile taking an initial qualitative pass in order to give an idea of the levels of risk and to identify those risks that are likely to be severe, with the objective of a more qualitative assessment later on.

Alternatively, a compromise solution often works well, since it can combine objective detail with subjective description. Instead of spending significant amounts of time in establishing the exact losses that might be incurred by a particular activity, the compromise solution takes a range of impact values and assigns descriptive terms to them. This is also known as semi-quantitative assessment.

So, for example, we might state that a in particular scenario, the term 'very low' approximates to values up to £25,000, 'low' to values between £25,000 and £250,000, 'medium' to values between £250,000 and £1 million, 'high' to values between £1 million and £25 million and, finally, 'very high' to values in excess of £25 million.

Although we have provided boundaries for the levels, there will be a degree of uncertainty about the upper and lower limits of each, but in general the ranges should be sufficient to provide a fairly subjective assessment whilst placing it in terms that the board will understand quickly. Clearly, these ranges will differ from one scenario to another, but set a common frame of reference when there are a substantial number of assessments to be carried out. These ranges should be agreed when setting the criteria for assessment.

For those situations in which there are no applicable financial values, such as reputational or operational impacts, a similar method of quantification can be used. Table 4.2 illustrates some possible options.

Table 4.2 Typical impact scales

Level of impact	Operational	Financial	Legal and regulatory	Reputational	Wellbeing
Very low	Partial loss of a single service	Loss of less than £25,000	Warning from regulatory body	Minor negative publicity	Inconvenience to several people
Low	Total loss of a single service	Loss between £25,000 and £250,000	Penalties up to £10,000	Local negative publicity	Injury or harm to one person
Medium	Partial loss of multiple services	Loss between £250,000 and £1 million	Penalties between £10,000 and £50,000	National negative publicity	Injury or harm to several people
High	Total loss of multiple services	Loss between £1 million and £25 million	Penalties between £50,000 and £500,000	EU-wide negative publicity	Loss of single life
Very high	Total loss of all services	Loss exceeds £25 million	Penalties exceed £500,000	Worldwide negative publicity	Multiple loss of life

Impact assessment questions

Let us take a look at the questions we need to ask when conducting an impact assessment. Note that a template form for this is included in Appendix F.

To begin with, apart from basic information such as name of department, name of contact(s) and contact details, for each information asset we will need to understand:

- the capital value of the asset, if it has one;
- the current and projected revenues the asset generates or contributes to;
- the value of any resources and activities required to maintain and support this asset, including:
  - staff;
  - systems hardware;

- systems operating system and application software;
- information such as databases, designs, etc;
- services, including third-party services;
- premises;
- other infrastructure.

- the required operational levels for each of these resources, in the short, medium and long term;
- how long the organisation can survive without these resources, expressed in minutes, hours, days or weeks (note that, in business continuity terms, this is often referred to as the maximum tolerable period of disruption, or MTPD);
- the impact on the information asset in terms of operational, financial, legal and regulatory, reputational and people impact;
- how long any relevant activities take to complete;
- what effect disruptions have on these activities and other activities within the business;
- what dependencies there are for activities to be completed.

Who should be involved in an impact assessment?

Clearly, the information asset owner should be the first port of call for this activity. However, although the information asset owner may be familiar with the technical details of the asset itself, he or she may not be able to express its value in business terms, so it is always worth double-checking with another person – or group of people – in the case of substantial information assets, such as a customer database, which may cut across several different areas of the organisation.

In larger organisations, it is quite possible that impact assessments may be carried out at three different levels, with the senior management team defining what information assets are critical to the organisation at a strategic level, departmental managers refining this assessment and identifying the individual components and operational managers making the final impact assessments themselves.

Strategic impact assessment

The strategic impact assessment begins with input from senior management who have a detailed high-level view of the organisation. They will be able to interpret the organisation's position in terms of both the internal and external contexts, and will appreciate the value of the customer base and the organisation's overall information assets.

The strategic impact assessment will determine which information assets are deemed to be essential to the survival of the organisation, and will make an initial estimate of the importance of each. This may well be modified in the tactical impact assessment when details of the information assets become clearer. If the organisation decides to omit any information assets from the impact assessment, the reasoning behind this decision should be clearly stated.

The strategic impact assessment should take into account the business-specific factors or general impact types that might affect the organisation, such as the interests of stakeholders, any statutory legal or regulatory obligations, the reputation of the organisation and its financial future. The organisation must begin by clearly defining at what point the level of impact constitutes a change from 'tolerable' to 'intolerable'.

When conducting a strategic impact assessment, each information asset should be separately investigated against each general impact type, and estimation made of the likely time that might elapse before it becomes business affecting, since loss if information assets may not be felt immediately. It is also useful at this stage to provide any reasoning for this, so a more objective analysis can be conducted, especially in cases where two or more information assets are considered, and the organisation feels it is desirable to prioritise one over the other.

Tactical impact assessment

Senior managers will undoubtedly have a general idea of what information assets are critical to the organisation, but may not have a detailed knowledge of their makeup or who is responsible for them, so, having agreed which information assets are being covered by the strategic impact assessment, we now turn to the tactical impact assessment and set the scope of this work.

In this case, we are less interested in the external context as this has already been addressed by the strategic business impact assessment, so we are now interested in those of the organisation's activities that contribute to the delivery of the organisation's products and services and any interdependencies between them. It may be extremely useful to piece together a block diagram illustrating this interdependence in order to simplify later work.

Operational impact assessment

Finally, we turn to the operation level of impact assessment, in which those managers having a detailed knowledge of, and responsibility for, the information asset provide an assessment of the actual potential impact of the asset's damage, loss or destruction.

Over- and underestimation

When carrying out impact and likelihood assessments, a mistake frequently made is either to overestimate or underestimate the realities of the situation. Often this is done with the best of intentions, but either can cause considerable difficulties later in the risk management process.

If overestimation takes place, more time, effort and money might be spent in treating risks than is necessary, or, indeed, the balance between the potential losses and the costs of treatment may change to make the correct form of risk treatment uneconomical.

Where underestimation occurs, risks that should be viewed as being more serious might well not be treated to a sufficient extent, or may be unwittingly accepted when avoidance, transfer or reduction might have been a more appropriate option.

Time dependency

Impacts can also change with and over time. Those threats that affect capital items – buildings, equipment and so on – will result in an instantaneous financial impact, whilst those that affect sales revenue streams, for example, will possibly show little impact at first, but over the course of days or weeks the impact would increase in a linear fashion. The other factor affecting this form of impact will be the hours during which the information must be available, since a system failure that occurs 'out of hours' may have no effect on revenue at all.

Figure 4.9 illustrates how the organisation might view the impact of financial losses over time.

Figure 4.9 Potential losses over time following a disruptive event

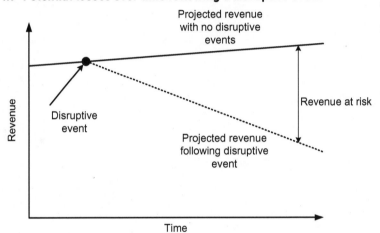

There are, of course, some times that are the worst possible for an incident to affect information assets. These include:

- regular events, such as end-of-month accounting dates;
- seasonal occasions, such as Easter, Christmas and summer holidays;
- heavy load occasions, such as the beginning of the school or university year.

Validating the results

Once the interviews or workshops have been completed, and the results of the questionnaires have been produced, they should be passed back to the originators for review and comment. They should be allowed time to consider their input and invited to verify the accuracy of the information before it is finalised for presentation.

A typical impact assessment form might look something like that shown in Figure 4.10.

Figure 4.10 Typical impact assessment form

Impact/Asset			Date	
Asset owner			Analyst	
Asset location			Reference	

	Primary impacts		Secondary impacts	
	Direct impacts	Indirect impacts	Direct impacts	Indirect impacts
Operational				
Score				
Legal and regulatory				
Score				
Reputational				
Score				
People-related				
Score				
Financial				
Score				
Total financial impact				
Total impact rating				

VH = Very High   H = High   M = Medium   L = Low   VL = Very Low

5 THREAT AND VULNERABILITY ASSESSMENT

In 2002, US Secretary of State Donald Rumsfeld said the following during a briefing:

> There are known knowns; there are things that we know that we know. We also know there are known unknowns; that is to say we know there are some things we do not know. But there are also unknown unknowns, the ones we don't know we don't know.

This is partly true of threats, but very true of vulnerabilities.

CONDUCTING THREAT ASSESSMENTS

Some experts believe that the threat and vulnerability assessments should be carried out ahead of the impact assessments; others disagree and opt for the reverse arrangement.

The author believes that, in practice, either method will suffice as long as the information assets have been clearly identified, but that it can be extremely helpful if the threat and vulnerability assessments can often be performed at the same time as impact assessments, since many of the threats and vulnerabilities will be apparent to the information asset owners. Further threat and vulnerability assessments can be conducted at a later time with other knowledgeable staff, especially with information security specialists.

For every threat identified, there may well also be some data on the frequency of historical events where the threat has either been known to have been used or to have succeeded.

It is also worthwhile remembering that a threat can only cause an impact on an information asset if the asset contains a vulnerability for the threat to exploit.

To begin with, it may well be worth running a brainstorming session to identify possible threats. In the first pass through, as with normal brainstorming rules, no suggestion should be discounted, no matter how bizarre it might seem, since sometimes those ideas that seem crazy at first glance turn out to be viable threats. The weeding out of the very unlikely threats can come at a later stage when the likelihood assessments are carried out.

It is worthwhile remembering, however, that even the most thorough threat assessment might not identify all the threats and hazards that the organisation faces, and also that new ones may emerge with time, so, as with all other aspects of an information risk management programme, this should be an ongoing activity.

Following the first pass through a brainstorming session, it may also be beneficial when conducting both threat and vulnerability assessments to use a mind map, so that all threats, hazards and vulnerabilities can be grouped, as shown in Figure 5.1.

The output of the threat assessment will include threats and hazards from a number of different sources including, but not limited to:

- malicious intrusion or hacking;
- environmental threats and hazards;
- errors and failures;
- social engineering;
- misuse and abuse;
- physical threats;
- malware.

These threats and hazards are described briefly below, and in greater detail in Appendix B.

Malicious intrusion or hacking

Hacking is a generic term applied to many forms of unpleasant behaviour, although it began as a description of what people did in order to find out how computers worked and how to improve their performance. Hacking almost invariably results in a breach of confidentiality, integrity or availability as hackers use software tools to intercept and decrypt legitimate information, and either steal it or change it. Occasionally, hacking is used to deliver so-called 'denial of service' (DoS) attacks, designed to prevent legitimate access to systems, often to make a political point.

Since the introduction of the CMA in 1990, hacking is now treated as a crime, since it invariably involves accessing a computer without the owner's permission to do so.

It is becoming more and more common to hear news stories about hackers who steal large quantities of information, such as user identifiers and passwords, and sell this information on – usually to criminal gangs – for use in wider fraud.

Recently, news broke regarding a successful hacking attack on eBay, in which more than 200 million people had their personal details stolen including telephone numbers, names, postal and email addresses, dates of birth and the passwords to their accounts. Of those, 15 million were eBay customers in the UK. It is somewhat ironic that eBay also owns PayPal, which is used to pay for many of the transactions on eBay itself; so what does this say about the security of our PayPal accounts?

Figure 5.1 Typical threats and hazards

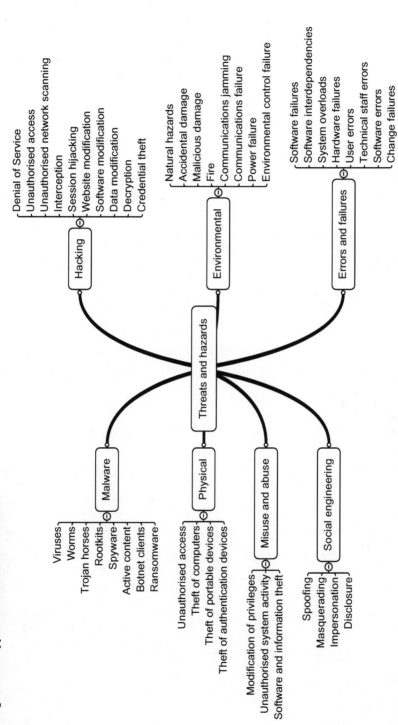

Hacking includes:

- DoS attacks;
- unauthorised access;
- unauthorised network scanning;
- interception;
- session hijacking;
- website modification;
- software modification;
- data modification;
- decryption;
- credential theft.

Environmental threats

These types of threat are almost always concerned with availability, since they affect the environment in which a system resides. Those threats that occur as a result of natural events – for example, severe weather – are often referred to as hazards in order to distinguish their motivation from those of malicious threats. Many of these hazards affect a wide geographic area, and can cause serious disruption to multiple organisations rather than to a specific organisation or system. Examples of environmental threats include:

- natural hazards such as severe weather and flooding;
- accidental and malicious physical damage;
- fire;
- communications jamming or interference;
- communications failures;
- power failures.

Errors and failures

Errors fall neatly into two categories – those made by users and technical staff, and those things that simply fail. Neither form is regarded as being malevolent, even though some user and technical errors are caused by lack of attention or poor training. Despite the view of many technicians that both hardware and software is designed to cause them grief, there is no evidence to suggest that this is actually the case. Examples of error threats include:

- software failures;
- software interdependencies;
- system overloads;

- hardware failures;
- user errors;
- technical staff errors;
- internal and external software errors;
- change failures.

Social engineering

Social engineering is a technique used by hackers and other ne'er-do-wells to acquire information, generally about access to systems so that their hacking activities are simplified. Social engineering comes in several forms – not only the traditional approach where a hacker attempts to engage with a user by conversation (usually over the telephone or by email), but also by disguising malware as legitimate software and web links and by copying the style-naming conventions and language of a target organisation. For example, they may send a user an email that appears to originate from their bank, as described in Chapter 1, but in which embedded web links take the user to the hacker's own website. Examples of social engineering threats include:

- spoofing, masquerading and impersonation;
- phishing;
- spam;
- disclosure.

Misuse and abuse

Whereas hacking is usually deemed to originate from outside an organisation, misuse normally originates from within. The net result may well be the same for either approach, but in the case of misuse, the internal user or technician has the added advantage of already being on the right side of the organisation's firewall and security systems, may have access to the required passwords and have suitable access privileges. For this reason, the threat from internal attackers potentially presents a significantly greater level of likelihood of success than that of an external attacker. Examples of misuse threats include:

- modification of privileges;
- unauthorised system activity;
- software and business information theft.

Physical threats

Many physical threats are also undertaken by employees – many will have access to systems and equipment that they can easily remove from the organisation's premises without the fear of discovery, whereas an external attacker would have to pass through the organisation's layers of physical security in order to do so.

There is a salutatory anecdote from the building trade that tells of the employee who pushed a wheelbarrow covered with a tarpaulin home at the end of the day's work. Every evening the site foreman checked beneath the tarpaulin to find there was nothing there and let the employee go on his way. Eventually, it was discovered that the man was stealing wheelbarrows and tarpaulins!

Physical threats include:

- unauthorised access;
- theft of computers and portable devices;
- theft of authentication devices.

Malware

The term 'malware' is used to refer to malicious software that can be used to attack an information system. Examples of malware include software entities that result in the collection of, damage to or removal of information. Such software is almost always concealed from the user; often self-replicating, attaching itself to an executable program, and can spread to other systems when the user unwittingly activates it.

Some malware goes to great lengths to conceal its existence, appearing to the user as legitimate software. Its purpose, however, is usually sinister in that it may collect, damage or remove information when the user activates what they believe is a legitimate program. Examples of malware include:

- viruses;
- worms;
- trojan horses;
- rootkits;
- spyware;
- active content;
- botnet clients;
- ransomware.

Who should be involved in a threat assessment?

As with the impact assessments covered in Chapter 4, the information asset owners should be the first port of call for this activity, since they may well already be aware of many of the threats their information assets face. However, other parts of the organisation will be able to provide input on this, such as the IT department, human resources and the organisation's information security team.

Additionally, there are comprehensive examples of threat types to be found in Appendix C of ISO/IEC 27005, including suggestions as to the origin of threats – accidental, deliberate and environmental – as well as the possible motivations and consequences of threats resulting from various types of threat source.

A typical threat assessment form might look something like that shown in Figure 5.2.

CONDUCTING VULNERABILITY ASSESSMENTS

Vulnerabilities are weaknesses in information assets, or in the infrastructure that underpins them, whilst threats exploit vulnerabilities in order to achieve an impact.

The output of the vulnerability assessment will include such vulnerabilities as:

- access control failures;
- systems acquisition, development and maintenance procedures;
- physical and environmental failures;
- communications and operations management failures;
- people-related security failures.

However, vulnerabilities alone cannot cause an impact on an information asset, as an impact requires the presence of a threat to exploit the vulnerability.

For every vulnerability identified, there may well also be some additional data on the whether the vulnerability has either been known to have been exploited, whether such exploits have succeeded, and whether there might be known controls that are already in place in partial mitigation.

As with threat assessments, it may well be worth running a brainstorming session to identify possible vulnerabilities, and in the first pass through, as with normal brainstorming rules, no suggestion should be discounted, no matter how bizarre it might seem, since sometimes those ideas that seem crazy at first glance turn out to be viable vulnerabilities. The weeding out of the very unlikely vulnerabilities can come at a later stage when the likelihood assessments are carried out.

It is worthwhile remembering, however, that even the most thorough vulnerability assessment might not identify all the vulnerabilities which affect the organisation's information assets, and also that new ones may emerge with time, so, as with all other aspects of an information risk management programme, this should be an ongoing activity.

Following the first pass through a brainstorming session, it may also be beneficial when conducting vulnerability assessments to use a mind map, so that all vulnerabilities can be grouped, as shown in Figure 5.3.

Figure 5.2 Typical threat assessment form

Date			Reference	
	Threat description			
Hacking				
Environmental threats and hazards				
Errors and failures				
Social engineering				
Misuse and abuse				
Physical threats				
Malware				
Operating systems affected				
Applications affected				
Information types affected				
Previous attack history (if known)				
Previous success rate (if known)				
Attack motivation (if known)				

Figure 5.3 Typical vulnerabilities

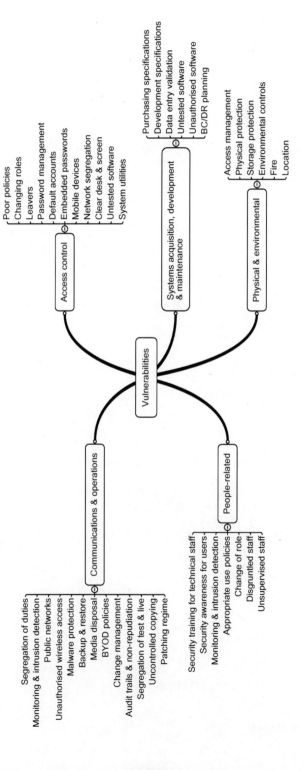

Typical vulnerabilities are described briefly below, and in greater detail in Appendix C.

Access control failures

Access control has two complementary uses – first, to permit access to resources for authorised persons and, second, to deny access to those resources to unauthorised persons. Failures in access control are very likely to increase the likelihood of successful attacks against information assets.

Appendix C4 of BS 7799-3 provides a highly comprehensive list of vulnerabilities, together with a brief description of how they might be exploited.

Access control failures include:

- the lack of, or poorly written, access control policies;
- failure to change the access rights of users changing role within the organisation;
- failure to revoke access rights of users leaving the organisation;
- inadequate user password management;
- the continued use of default system accounts and passwords;
- the use of passwords embedded in software applications;
- the lack of security of mobile devices;
- the lack of network segregation;
- failure to impose a clear desk and clear screen policy;
- the use of untested software;
- failure to restrict the use of system utilities.

Poor systems acquisition, development and maintenance procedures

When acquiring systems hardware and software, developing software and maintaining both, it is vital to ensure that selection is carried out according to a formal set of criteria that include appropriate security features. Unlike access control failures, this type of vulnerability is rarely noticed immediately but can result in serious consequences at a later time.

The root cause of this is often a failure to specify correctly appropriate criteria prior to acquisition or development, and may result either from a lack of forethought or a desire to achieve cost savings.

This type of vulnerability includes:

- the lack of clear functional purchasing specifications;
- the lack of clear functional development specifications;
- failure to validate data entry;
- the use of untested software;

- the use of unauthorised software;
- the lack or BC/DR planning.

Physical and environmental failures

Physical security is normally highly visible, both to staff and to potential intruders. Very often, the mere presence of robust security is sufficient to deter an intruder, but even so it is important that physical security measures are appropriate and well maintained, and failure to do this increases the organisation's likelihood of experiencing intrusion of some description.

Environmental vulnerabilities tend to be rather more difficult to address but are generally relatively easy to identify and can either relate to the location or construction of premises (for example in a flood plain), or to the environmental subsystems that underpin major premises such as large office buildings, factories, warehouses and data centres.

Physical and environmental vulnerabilities include:

- poor management of access to premises and to areas within them;
- inadequate physical protection for premises, doors and windows;
- the lack of suitable protection for stored equipment and supplies, and especially waste;
- the use of unsuitable environmental systems, including cooling and humidity control;
- the location of premises in areas prone to flooding;
- the uncontrolled storage of flammable or hazardous materials;
- the location of premises in proximity to flammable or hazardous materials or facilities that process them.

Communications and operations management failures

Along with access control failures, failures of operations management and communications systems rank high among the vulnerabilities that can be successfully exploited, whether deliberately or accidentally. Many of these exploits are possible due to process failures – again, either through failure to observe them or to have them in the first place.

Communications and operations management failures include:

- the failure to ensure the appropriate segregation of duties where necessary;
- inadequate network monitoring and management, including intrusion detection;
- the use of unprotected public networks;
- the uncontrolled use of users' own wireless access points;
- poor protection against malware, and failure to keep protection up to date;
- failure to maintain patching of software;

- inadequate and untested backup and restoral procedures;
- improper disposal of 'end of life' storage media;
- the lack of robust 'Bring Your Own Device' (BYOD) policies;
- inadequate change management procedures;
- the lack of audit trails, non-repudiation of transactions and email messages;
- the lack of segregation of test and production systems;
- the uncontrolled copying of business information.

People-related security failures

Finally, we look at those vulnerabilities that are caused by the failures of users and operational staff. These are almost all related to policies and processes:

- the insufficient or inappropriate security training of technical staff;
- the lack of appropriate security awareness training for users;
- the lack of monitoring mechanisms, including intrusion detection systems;
- the lack of robust policies for the correct and appropriate use of systems, communications, media, social networking and messaging;
- the failure to review users' access rights whenever they change roles or leave the organisation;
- the lack of a procedure to ensure the return of assets when leaving the organisation;
- unmotivated or disgruntled staff;
- unsupervised work by third-party organisations or by staff who work outside normal business hours.

Who should be involved in a vulnerability assessment?

As with the threat assessments covered earlier in this chapter, the information asset owners should be the first port of call for this activity, since they may well already be aware of many of the vulnerabilities their information assets already possess. However, other parts of the organisation will be able to provide input on this, such as the IT department, human resources and the organisation's information security team.

Since many of the vulnerabilities identified will be of a technical nature, it is probable that various forms of security testing will identify them, including penetration testing and vulnerability scanning tools.

Additionally, there are comprehensive examples of vulnerability types to be found in Appendix D of ISO/IEC 27005, including suggestions as to the types of threat that could exploit them.

A typical impact assessment form might look something like that shown in Figure 5.4.

Figure 5.4 Typical vulnerability assessment form

Date		Reference	
	Vulnerability description		
Access control			
Systems acquisition, development and maintenance			
Physical and environmental			
People-related			
Communications and operations			
Operating systems affected			
Applications affected			
Information types affected			
Previous attack history (if known)			
Previous success rate (if known)			
Attack motivation (if known)			

IDENTIFICATION OF EXISTING CONTROLS

Before we can move on to the next stage of risk assessment, we must identify all existing controls that are in place and also verify that they are working as expected. There are three reasons for doing this:

- First, to ensure that when we conduct the likelihood assessment, we have all the necessary information to do so accurately.

- Second, to ensure that when we begin the process of determining the appropriate controls to mitigate the risks we have encountered, we do not duplicate controls that are already in place, and that they are effective and are functioning as expected.

- Third, so that any controls that are not effective or functioning as expected can be reviewed and removed or replaced as necessary.

If the organisation has already been through one complete information risk management programme, then the information to complete this activity will be in the risk register. If, however, this is the first time it has been conducted, the identification of existing controls will have to be carried out from scratch.

We deal with controls in much greater detail in Chapter 7, but in order to assist the identification process for this stage of the work, the following should prove useful.

Controls are divided into four strategic, four tactical and three operational types, but not all combinations of these exist. Strategic controls are:

- Avoid or terminate – i.e. either cease an activity that incurs risk or do not begin it.

- Transfer or share – i.e. spread the risk between the organisation and one or more third parties.

- Reduce or modify – i.e. change either the impact or the likelihood in some way.

- Accept or tolerate – when the other options cannot treat the risk, this is the one choice remaining.

Tactical controls are:

- Detective – i.e. being alerted to something happening.

- Preventative – i.e. stopping something from happening.

- Directive – i.e. putting in place some form of instruction.

- Corrective – i.e. altering the state or condition of something.

Operational controls are:

- Physical or environmental – these are usually concerned with the infrastructure that underpins the information assets. Typical examples of physical controls are the use of CCTV to monitor areas within a site, and electronic door locking mechanisms to control access into restricted areas.

- Procedural or people – these are concerned with ensuring that processes and procedures are followed. Typical examples of procedural controls are change control mechanisms to manage additional systems or services, and the segregation of duties that could otherwise result in fraud.

- Technical or logical – these are usually concerned with hardware and software in some form. Typical examples of technical controls include the use of anti-virus software to quarantine or delete malware, and firewalls to block unauthorised network intrusion.

These controls are all illustrated in Figure 5.5.

Who should be involved in the identification of existing controls?

As with the threat and vulnerability assessments covered earlier in this chapter, the information asset owners should be the first port of call for this activity, since they may well already be aware of many of the controls already present for their information assets. However, other parts of the organisation will be able to provide input on this, such as the IT department, human resources and the organisation's information security team.

A typical controls identification form might look something like that shown in Figure 5.6.

Figure 5.5 The overall scheme of risk treatment options

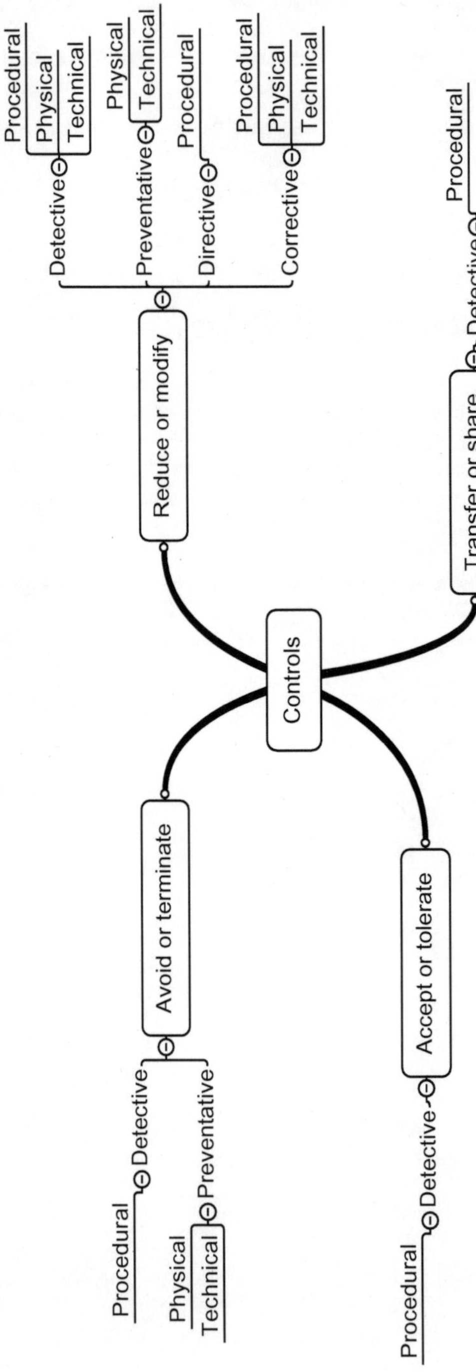

Figure 5.6 Typical existing controls identification form

Date			Reference	
Description of controls				
Asset name				
Asset location				
Preventative controls	Physical or environmental			
	Technical or logical			
Detective controls	Physical or environmental			
	Technical or logical			
	Procedural or people			
Directive controls	Procedural or people			
Corrective controls	Physical or environmental			
	Technical or logical			
	Procedural or people			

6   RISK ANALYSIS AND RISK EVALUATION

The process of risk assessment continues with risk analysis, in which we develop an understanding of the risks. We begin by identifying the likelihood or probability of a threat or hazard having an impact on an information asset, and using that impact assessment we calculate the overall level of risk.

In risk identification, we examined the general impacts or consequences faced by an information asset, then the threats that might cause them, followed by any vulnerabilities they might possess. These three assessments were carried out in isolation, since at that stage of the risk management process the relationship between them did not matter.

In risk analysis, however, we bring the three assessments together, along with any controls already implemented and examine the impacts that occur to information assets as a result of specific threat events. This may also require an understanding of any motivations that might exist for deliberate incidents.

First, we assess how likely it is for any given threat or hazard to exploit a vulnerability and cause harm to an information asset.

ASSESSMENT OF LIKELIHOOD

As mentioned in Chapter 5, the likelihood of a threat taking advantage of a vulnerability to cause harm to an information asset will depend on a number of factors, including:

- the value of the asset to the attacker, which is usually, but not always, financial; the history of previously successful attacks; the risk of an attacker being detected either during or following an attack, whether successful or not; and the complexity of the attack;

- the motivation of the attacker, which is sometimes financial or sometimes the result of a grievance; the skills and tools required to carry out the attack; the level of any vulnerabilities within the information asset, including how well they are known; and the presence or otherwise of existing controls.

Clearly, for environmental hazards, errors and failures, the concept of an attacker has no meaning, but for the other forms of threat described – physical threats, malicious intrusion or hacking, misuse and abuse, malware – an attacker will be present in some form, and this will have a profound effect on the likelihood of the attack succeeding.

An attacker may simply wish to steal the information asset or make a copy of it. This is straightforward theft, and, hence, has a confidentiality impact. Alternatively, the attacker may wish to alter the information asset to gain some benefit – a higher grade, for example; or to reduce the benefit to the information owner, perhaps because of some perceived grievance; or to cause customer dissatisfaction. These have an integrity impact on the information asset. Finally, the attacker may wish to deny the information owner or the owner's customers rightful access to the information asset, again possibly because of some perceived grievance, and this is an availability impact.

Clearly, the greater the motivation an attacker has, the greater will be the likelihood of the attack being successful, and possibly also the greater the impact on the information asset.

However, likelihood or probability can still be extremely difficult things to rate. Many of the events we will consider occur 'as and when', rather than at pre-defined intervals, and so we are unable to determine exactly when a particular incident is likely to occur. Estimation is therefore the order of the day, but we need to take care with our approach so that it is both meaningful and consistent.

As with the assessment of impact, we turn to the two possible methods of likelihood assessment – qualitative and quantitative.

Qualitative and quantitative assessments – which should we use?

Qualitative assessments are almost always subjective. The terms 'low', 'medium' and 'high' give a general indication of the likelihood of an event occurring, but do not tell us how likely. Quantitative assessments, on the other hand, can be very specific and rather more accurate. The main problem with quantitative assessments is that, if they are to be entirely accurate, they can take a great deal of time to undertake and, mostly, total accuracy is not a requirement.

In the case of likelihood assessment, it may be worthwhile taking an initial qualitative pass in order to give an idea of the levels of risk and to identify those risks that are likely to be severe, with the objective of a more quantitative assessment later on.

Alternatively, a compromise solution often works well, since it can combine objective detail with subjective description. Instead of spending significant amounts of time in establishing the exact likelihood of a particular event, the compromise solution takes a range of impact values and assigns descriptive terms to them. This is also known as semi-quantitative assessment.

So, for example, we might state that in a particular scenario, the term 'very unlikely' approximates to an event that occurs once in a decade; 'unlikely' to one that occurs once a year; 'possible' to one that occurs once a month; 'likely' to one that occurs once a week; and 'very likely' to one that might occur at any time.

Although we have provided boundaries for the levels, there will be a degree of uncertainty about the upper and lower limits of each, but in general the ranges should be sufficient to provide a fairly subjective assessment whilst placing it in terms that the board will understand quickly. Clearly, these ranges will differ from one scenario to another, but set a common frame of reference when there are a substantial number of assessments to be carried out. These ranges should be agreed when setting the criteria for assessment.

Fully quantitative assessment relies on our being able to predict the probability of an event occurring based on the likely frequency of it doing so. This requires a knowledge or experience of statistics, which is outside the scope of this book, but unless probability information is available and deemed to be trustworthy, frequency is unlikely to yield reliable results.

Historical data may be useful in providing an initial assessment and in developing appropriate likelihood scales, but it is important to base these on sufficient data so that the results are meaningful, since too little data will almost certainly provide a skewed view of likelihood.

Another problem that increases the uncertainty of likelihood assessments is that of proximity. Just because an event occurs (statistically) once every 10 years does not mean that it will not occur in two successive years or, conversely, that it will occur at all in the next 20.

If quantitative assessment proves to be too challenging, we may opt instead for qualitative assessment. However, as with impact assessment, qualitative likelihood assessment tends to be very subjective, and the terms 'highly unlikely' and 'almost certain' mean little except to the person who sets them.

In order to provide a more objective likelihood assessment, we might combine a qualitative scale with quantitative values, as we suggested with impact assessment, so that we can place each assessment on a meaningful basis.

For example, severe cold weather-related events tend to be more common in the winter months whilst others, such as extreme flooding, may only occur once in every few years and at any time of year. The Environment Agency in the UK provides estimates of the possible depth of floodwater, but, as always, these are only estimates and neither the extent of flooding nor the frequency at which it might occur can be relied upon for accurate likelihood determination. The timeframe scale for this kind of event might therefore range from months to decades. Alternatively, hacking attempts can and do occur much more frequently, and so a timeframe scale for these will be rather different.

The likelihood of whichever kind of threat or hazard we face must therefore be judged against an appropriate scale devised as part of the setting of general risk management criteria, and if the worst-case scenario is used for likelihood assessments, this should ideally be the standard for all.

An example of possible likelihood scales for the different categories of threats described earlier is shown in Table 6.1.

The final stage in the assessment of likelihood is to place it against each threat identified earlier in the risk identification process, so that we can begin the next stage – risk analysis.

Table 6.1 Typical likelihood scales

Level of likelihood	Hacking, malware and social engineering	Environmental	Errors, failures, misuse and physical
Very unlikely	The event is likely to occur once a week	The event is likely to occur once a decade	The event is likely to occur once a month
Unlikely	The event is likely to occur once a day	The event is likely to occur once a year	The event is likely to occur once a week
Possible	The event is likely to occur several times a day	The event is likely to occur once a month	The event is likely to occur once a day
Likely	The event is likely to occur several times an hour	The event is likely to occur weekly	The event is likely to occur several times a day
Very likely	The event is likely to occur at any time	The event is likely to occur at any time	The event is likely to occur at any time

RISK ANALYSIS

Once we have assessed the impact or consequence of an incident, and also the likelihood of it occurring, we are in a position to analyse the risk. Typically, this is carried out using a risk matrix of the type shown in Figure 6.1.

Figure 6.1 A typical risk matrix

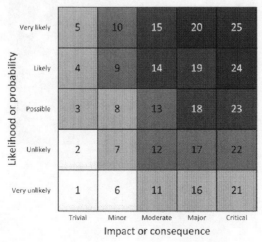

A risk matrix is simply a tool to assist in the ranking of risks in terms of overall severity, and in order to help prioritise the assessed risks for treatment. Since it is purely a visual representation of the risks identified, it should only be used at the very end of the risk assessment process, once both the impact and the likelihood have been assessed.

Since we will have been consistent in using scales that truly represent the impact and the likelihood regardless of the type of threat, we can safely plot every impact and likelihood assessment on the matrix in which a simple scale of 1 to 25 is defined.

If there are a number of risks assessed, it may be helpful to number them in some way so as to avoid too much clutter on the risk matrix itself. This allows us to prioritise the risks into five different rankings:

1. These are very low risks, and we can probably accept them.
2. These risks are not urgent, but may require treatment.
3. These risks are worth treatment.
4. These risks are important and require treatment.
5. These risks require urgent treatment.

However, this presents a rather simplistic view of risks when it comes to later prioritisation since, if we are dealing with a very large number of risks, a significant number could be ranked as urgent, and we would have no easy way of prioritising them for treatment. For that reason we might instead use an enhanced risk matrix, in which a slightly altered scale of 1 to 25 is defined, and some bias is given to those risks that are more likely to occur, as shown in Figure 6.2.

Figure 6.2 An enhanced risk matrix

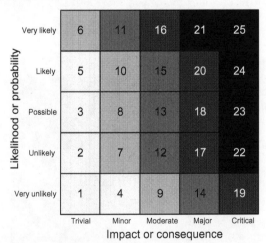

We will now be in a position to record the risk ranking value and begin prioritising the risks for treatment. The next stage in this process is to transfer everything we know about the risks to a risk register.

RISK EVALUATION

Risk evaluation – in which the various risks analysed are transferred onto a risk register, and agreement is reached on which risks require treatment and examine how this should be achieved.

The risk register

The risk register is a method of tracking all risks identified within the information risk management programme, regardless of whether or not they are able to be treated by avoidance, transfer or reduction, or to be accepted.

There is no set structure for a risk register, but it should be remembered that 'less is more', and that too much information can render the risk register unusable. It is better, therefore, to record only the very necessary information in the risk register and to provide links – possibly hyperlinks – to any background information. The following information is necessary and sufficient for completeness:

- a risk reference number, possibly prefixed by the organisation's department name;
- the date the entry was added to the risk register;
- the name of the information asset;
- the name of the asset owner;
- a brief description of the risk it faces;
- the level of impact assessed;
- the likelihood assessed;
- the resulting risk level;
- the recommended operational control(s);
- the name of the person responsible for implementing the control(s);
- the date by which the controls should be in place;
- the next review date for the risk.

It may also be desirable to indicate whether the control(s) have been successful.

Some organisations develop an SQL database to act as a risk register, since this can be made prescriptive in terms of who may make changes, and how and when the entries are made or changed; smaller organisations often find that a simple spreadsheet is sufficient for their needs as shown in Figure 6.3.

Figure 6.3 A typical risk register spreadsheet

Information Risk Register

Reference	Date added	Asset name	Asset owner	Brief description of risk	Inherent risk			Treatment *	Recommended control(s)	Control owner	Date due	Residual risk			Next review date
					Impact	Likelihood	Risk level					Impact	Likelihood	Risk level	

Treatment: X = Avoid; S = Share; R = Reduce; A = Accept

There is, however, a major caveat when it comes to sharing the risk register. The register itself becomes an information asset, and may contain information that could be detrimental to the organisation if it were to become publicly available, since it provides a comprehensive list of all the organisation's information assets and the risks they face. Therefore, the risk register should be protected with its own set of controls and only shared with those people within the organisation who have a genuine need to see it.

It will be clear at this point that some fields within the register cannot yet be completed, since we have not actually conducted the risk evaluation. This is the next and final stage in the risk assessment process.

Risk evaluation

In the process of risk evaluation, we take each risk in turn and compare it with the risk criteria, which is covered in Chapter 3.

We begin by comparing the potential impact or consequence with the organisation's risk appetite for that particular information asset. If the impact is less than the level set as the risk appetite, the organisation may decide to accept the risk, but to record the fact and ensure that the risk is monitored over time in case either its impact or likelihood changes.

Next, we compare the risks with the risk treatment criteria – also established in Chapter 3 – to decide on the most appropriate form of risk treatment, which includes risk avoidance or termination, risk transfer or sharing, risk reduction or modification, and risk acceptance or tolerance.

The recommendation at this stage of the process will only be which of the strategic options the organisation should employ and will not go down to the tactical or operational level, since this is part of the risk treatment process.

Some organisations assist the recommendation process by introducing three separate bands of risk:

- an upper band in which the level of risk is regarded as being intolerable, regardless of the costs or complexities of treatment;
- a middle band in which the cost/benefit of treatment is considered along with other risk appetite criteria;
- a lower band, in which the level risk is so low that it can clearly be accepted or tolerated.

We should also remember that, although any of these choices might reduce the risk to a level below that of the organisation's risk appetite, it may well be possible to reduce it further by employing more than one of the risk treatment options, and, in addition to recommending which methods to employ, the organisation may also need to consider in which order they should be employed.

Again, at this point in the process it may become clear that either the risk appetite criteria or the risk treatment criteria are insufficiently well defined to allow the organisation to make an informed decision as to the most appropriate form of risk treatment, since at the time, too little may have been known about the exact nature of the risks. These criteria may therefore require refinement, and the evaluation process must be repeated.

Likewise, there may be risks for which the recommended option still remains unclear, and in such cases the recommendation might be to conduct a further and more detailed risk assessment in order to better understand the risk and to make a more informed choice as to the method of treatment.

The recommendations should also provide some indication of the likely cost of treatment, since, if the cost outweighs the benefit, the organisation may decide to accept the risk as being too expensive to treat. As with any other accepted risk, this should be documented and monitored over time.

Whilst recommendations on risk treatment tend to be based upon the acceptable level of risk for each information asset, it is important that the evaluation process takes into account three key attributes:

- the aggregation of a number of lower-level risks, which may result in significantly higher overall risk;
- the importance to the organisation of any information asset when compared to others;
- the need to consider whether legal, regulatory and contractual risks might be more damaging to the organisation than others.

The output of the risk evaluation process will be:

- whether or not a risk requires treatment, and if so, which strategic option(s) are recommended;
- a prioritised list of the risks identified for treatment;
- an updated risk register, reflecting the recommendations made.

It would be normal practice at this point to submit a proposal for the overall risk treatment plan to senior management for consideration, together with any business cases required for treating those risks for which the cost exceeds a set threshold, again defined as part of the criteria for the information risk management programme.

The component parts of a business case are described in greater detail in Chapter 7.

7 RISK TREATMENT

Now we have completed the risk assessment process, it is time to begin to consider how to deal with the risks we have identified. The actions we take to treat risk are referred to as controls.

A control is any measure or action that modifies risk. Controls include any policy, procedure, practice, process, technology and technique, method or device that modifies or manages risk. Risk treatments either become controls, or modify existing controls, once they have been implemented.

Controls are the tools we use to take a level of inherent risk and modify it to a level that falls within the organisation's risk appetite, at which point the organisation is willing to accept the residual risk.

This chapter begins by taking an overview of the principle options for risk treatment. First, at the strategic risk treatment level, we have four options:

- to avoid or terminate the risk;
- to transfer or share the risk;
- to reduce or modify the risk;
- to accept or tolerate the risk.

At the end of this process, there may remain some 'residual' risk that we cannot treat, simply because we have exhausted all other possibilities or because the cost of further treatment would be more costly than the financial losses if the risk came to fruition. In this case, we must accept this residual risk, but subject it to ongoing monitoring.

In Chapter 3, we discussed the criteria for information risk management, and noted that there is a level of risk for each type of information asset, known as the risk appetite, above which the organisation will wish to treat the risk, and so it is important to understand that there will be situations in which more than one choice of treatment must be made in order to take the level of risk to a point that is acceptable to the organisation and bring it below the risk appetite level.

Next, for each strategic risk treatment option, there are one or more tactical options:

- detective controls;
- corrective controls;

- preventative controls;
- directive controls.

Finally, at the operational level, we have three types of control:

- physical controls;
- procedural controls;
- technical controls.

Figure 7.1 illustrates all the possible combinations of risk treatment, and we shall deal with each of these in turn, but, for the moment, let us look at the start of the process for deciding which strategic option or options are most suitable.

STRATEGIC RISK OPTIONS

Strategic risk management controls themselves do not actually treat the risk, but set the approach for treatment, rather like giving travel directions – 'head north/south/east/west'.

Figure 7.2 illustrates the process for determining the most appropriate strategic risk option.

Risk avoidance or termination

First, we will examine whether or not we can avoid or terminate the risk. This implies either not commencing an activity that would incur risk or to cease doing it if it has already commenced.

For example, if the organisation were considering building a new data centre and we had identified that there was a significant risk due to the building site being within a known flood plain, we would recommend that the organisation found a more suitable location. As long as the organisation accepted this recommendation, that particular risk would be terminated immediately.

As a slightly different example, if the organisation were in the process of moving large amounts of information to a Cloud service provider, and we had identified that this would place the organisation's confidential customer information in a jurisdiction that does not meet the requirements of the DPA,, we would recommend that the project be halted.

This would terminate that particular risk, but there would be two secondary impacts resulting from a decision to stop the project. First, there would be some cost for any work that had already been carried out, and possibly some contractual penalties, and, second, the organisation would be left with the problem of finding a replacement Cloud service supplier if it still wished to outsource the information, and again there would be a cost involved in doing this.

Figure 7.1 The overall scheme of risk treatment options

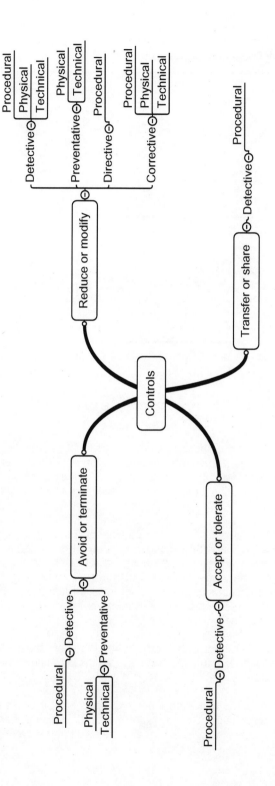

Figure 7.2 The strategic risk management process

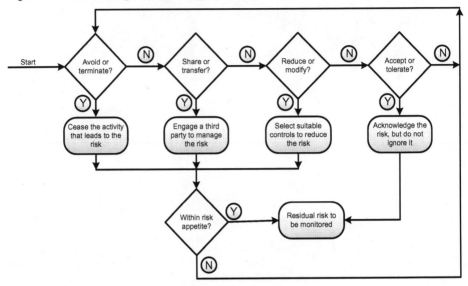

Risk transfer or sharing

If terminating the risk is not an option, the next option is to decide whether the risk can be transferred or shared with a third party.

This might seem to be a simple way of disposing of a risk, but it is not as straightforward as it may first appear. Whilst an organisation may transfer or share the actual treatment of the risk to a third party, the responsibility and accountability for the risk remains with the organisation, and in some situations it may not be possible to transfer or share the entire amount of the risk.

An example of the first of these possibilities would be where an organisation places its confidential customer information with a Cloud service provider whose systems are attacked by hackers and the information is made public. Although the outsourcing organisation would almost certainly have a legitimate claim of negligence against the Cloud service provider, the responsibility for the information leakage would still lie with the organisation, and the Information Commissioner would expect to penalise the organisation itself rather than the Cloud service provider.

So, although the risk has been shared, there remain a number of issues that the organisation faces, including secondary and indirect risks. All these must be taken into account when transferring risk.

An example of the second instance might be where an organisation takes out an insurance policy against the revenue losses incurred if their information systems fail. An insurance company might be happy to take on the entire risk, but the premiums to cover all possible losses might exceed the organisation's budget.

In order to reduce the premiums to an acceptable level, apart from demanding a number of guarantees such as fully tested DR systems, the insurer might well set an upper limit on the possible pay out in the event of a claim, so the organisation would be faced with accepting some residual risk.

Risk reduction or modification

In the past, this was often referred to as risk treatment, but the definition has now become more precise so as to avoid confusion with other forms of treatment.

When an organisation examines the possibilities for reducing or modifying risk, it means reducing the impact; reducing the likelihood or, more usually, a combination of both, since there are a number of different approaches to this at tactical and operational levels that may be used in combination to bring the level of risk down to below the organisation's level of risk appetite.

One typical example of risk reduction would be to reduce the likelihood of unauthorised remote access by replacing user ID and password authentication with two-factor authentication using a smartcard or security token as well as the existing user ID and password. This would strengthen the authentication process considerably and reduce the likelihood of a successful intrusion, but the organisation would then have to balance this benefit against the costs of deployment and ongoing support, plus the additional risk that a lost or stolen token could present a new threat.

Another example would be to reduce the impact of theft of a company laptop by encrypting the entire hard drive. The capital value of the laptop would still have been lost – although the risk of this might have been reduced under an insurance policy – but the information contained on the laptop would be secured and almost impossible for the thief to recover. Again, organisations might have to accept some residual risk – the replacement cost of the laptop in this example would be covered, but there would be some additional expenditure in configuring it.

Risk acceptance or tolerance

The final strategic option is to accept or tolerate the risk. Ordinarily this only happens when a risk is too costly to treat by any other means, or following other forms of risk treatment has reached a point where no further treatment is possible.

The most important aspect of risk acceptance is that it differs entirely from ignoring risk, which should never be an option under any circumstances. Accepted risks must always be documented as such and reviewed either at intervals, in case the level of risk has changed in the meantime, or if there has been a sudden change in either the threat or the likelihood that produced the risk in the first place.

Not all forms of strategic control involve the use of all forms of tactical control. For example, risk avoidance only ever involves detective or preventative controls, and never directive or corrective.

TACTICAL RISK MANAGEMENT CONTROLS

Using the earlier analogy, tactical risk management controls are similar to suggesting 'take the motorway as far as junction 20'. They consist of four different types – detective, preventative, directive and corrective.

As with strategic controls, tactical controls themselves do not actually treat the risks, but determine a more specific course of action.

Detective controls

Detective controls are those controls that advise or warn the organisation that an incident is taking place, but that is all they do – they themselves do not change either the impact or the likelihood of any risk, but operate alongside other types of tactical controls.

If action needs to be taken as a result of the warning, then this must necessarily be as a separate control (probably corrective), initiated either automatically by the detecting system or by a member of staff who is alerted by the warning. An example of a detective control is an alarm generated when an intruder forces open a security gate or door.

Preventative controls

Preventative controls are designed to stop an incident from taking place before it has begun. The choice of operational control will determine the actual steps to be taken, but preventative controls will ultimately reduce or eliminate the likelihood of an incident occurring, and will therefore reduce or terminate the risk. An example of a preventative control is the lock on a door or window giving access to an area to which an intruder might otherwise have free access.

Directive controls

Directive controls are totally instruction-based. They comprise policies, procedures, processes and works instructions, all of which dictate what must or must not be done.

As with detective controls, directive controls do not change either the impact or the likelihood of an incident occurring, since they only dictate policy. If people follow the policies, then the controls are successful, but if they do not, the controls will not be effective. For this reason, many organisations like to couple directive controls with other types, such as preventative or corrective, in order to enforce the policies. An example of a directive control would be a policy stating that passwords must be changed every 90 days – this could be enforced by a control within the computer's operating system that forces users to update their passwords at that interval.

Corrective controls

Corrective controls are those that, through appropriate operational controls, will make a difference either to the impact or to the likelihood of a risk. Corrective controls are invariably introduced after an event of some kind has occurred, and their purpose is to fix the problem.

Not all forms of tactical control involve all forms of operational control. For example, directive tactical controls only ever involve the use of procedural operational controls.

OPERATIONAL RISK MANAGEMENT CONTROLS

Using the earlier analogy, operational risk management controls are similar to providing more detailed directions to the destination, such as, 'Now take the A4303 east, then the A426 south for 2.5 miles'.

They come in just three varieties – procedural, physical and technical, also known sometimes as people, environmental and logical controls, respectively. As with tactical controls, operational controls may be used singly, or in conjunction with others in order to minimise a risk.

Procedural controls

Procedural controls, as the name suggests, simply put procedures in place to set out actions that users and technical staff must or must not take in any given circumstance. Procedural controls on their own do not change either the impact or the likelihood of a risk, but do so only where users follow them.

An example of a procedural control is that of a clear desk policy stating that users must leave no materials (for example, books or papers) on their desk when out of the office. This is in fact a directive/procedural control.

Physical controls

Physical controls are those that address physical and environmental threats, and as such always change either the impact or the likelihood of the risk. Physical controls may contain a technology element, but this is invariably unrelated to the information itself, merely pertaining to a technical solution to a physical risk. An example of a physical control (actually detective/physical) would be that of a closed-circuit television (CCTV) system to monitor the perimeter of a building.

Technical controls

Technical controls refer generally to those controls that are directly related to the technology that underpins (or is) the information-supporting infrastructure. Technical controls may be implemented either in hardware or in software, and frequently both. An example of a corrective/technical control is that of configuring a Virtual Local Area Network (VLAN) environment in order to segregate live and test networks.

EXAMPLES OF CRITICAL CONTROLS AND CONTROL CATEGORIES

The following sections list the chief controls suggested by:

- The Council on CyberSecurity Critical Security Controls Version 5.0.
- ISO/IEC 27001:2013.
- NIST Special Publication 800-53 Revision 4.

The Council on CyberSecurity Critical Security Controls Version 5.0

A number of organisations, including the UK's CPNI, have published a list of the 20 most critical security controls (see Figure 7.3). This is based upon The Council on CyberSecurity Critical Security Controls Version 5.0.

Figure 7.3 Council on CyberSecurity critical security controls

No.	Control title
1	Inventory of authorised and unauthorised devices
2	Inventory of authorised and unauthorised software
3	Secure configurations for hardware and software on mobile devices, laptops, workstations and servers
4	Continuous vulnerability assessment and remediation
5	Malware defences
6	Application software security
7	Wireless access control
8	Data recovery capability
9	Security skills assessment and appropriate training to fill gaps
10	Secure configurations for network devices such as firewalls, routers and switches
11	Limitation and control of network ports, protocols and services
12	Controlled use of administrative privileges
13	Boundary defence
14	Maintenance, monitoring and analysis of audit logs
15	Control access based on the need to know
16	Account monitoring and control
17	Data protection
18	Incident response and management
19	Secure network engineering
20	Penetration tests and red team exercises

Whilst this is not a comprehensive list of controls, it does provide a good starting point for organisations that have conducted their risk assessments, but are unsure where to begin with risk treatment. These controls are described more fully in Appendix D.

ISO/IEC 27001 controls

Although the primary ISO Standard for information risk management is ISO/IEC 27005, it contains no detailed information on suitable tactical or operational controls for risk treatment, restricting itself instead to the strategic level only. Instead, ISO/IEC 27001 provides a comprehensive list of 114 separate operational level controls, grouped into 14 categories (see Figure 7.4) in its Appendix A. A more detailed description of the controls can be found in ISO/IEC 27002 in its sections 5 to 18.

These control categories are expanded and described more fully in Appendix D.

Figure 7.4 ISO/IEC 27001 control categories

No.	Title (number of controls)
A.5	Information security policies (2)
A.6	Organisation of information security (7)
A.7	Human resource security (6)
A.8	Asset management (10)
A.9	Access control (14)
A.10	Cryptography (2)
A.11	Physical and environmental security (15)
A.12	Operations security (14)
A.13	Communications security (7)
A.14	System acquisition, development and maintenance (13)
A.15	Supplier relationships (5)
A.16	Information security incident management (7)
A.17	Information security aspects of business continuity management (4)
A.18	Compliance (8)

NIST Special Publication 800-53 Revision 4

Although the primary NIST publication on information risk management is Special Publication 800-30, it contains no detailed information on risk treatment or the selection of controls. NIST Special Publication 800-53 Revision 4 lists 256 separate operational level controls, grouped into 18 categories (see Figure 7.5) in its Appendix F, and also maps them against ISO/IEC 27001 controls in its Appendix H.

These control categories are expanded and described more fully in Appendix D.

Figure 7.5 NIST SP 800-53 control categories

Identifier	Family (number of controls)
AC	Access Control (25)
AT	Awareness and Training (5)
AU	Audit and Accountability (16)
CA	Security Assessment and Authorisation (9)
CM	Configuration Management (11)
CP	Contingency Planning (13)
IA	Identification and Authentication (11)
IR	Incident Response (10)
MA	Maintenance (6)
MP	Media Protection (8)
PE	Physical and Environmental Protection (20)
PL	Planning (9)
PS	Personnel Security (8)
RA	Risk Assessment (6)
SA	System and Services Acquisition (22)
SC	System and Communications Protection (44)
SI	System and Information Integrity (17)
PM	Program Management (16)

8 RISK REPORTING AND PRESENTATION

The process of communicating within the information risk management programme is extremely important, and serves a number of purposes. It allows the information risk management programme manager to:

- maintain a two-way flow of information between the programme manager and those stakeholders who are closely involved in the process of impact, threat and vulnerability assessments;
- keep the organisation's senior management and other stakeholders informed of general progress;
- flag up any risks deemed to be very severe, and which require immediate attention;
- present business cases requesting approval of recommendations and funding;
- report on those risks that have been successfully treated and those that remain untreated.

It is often said that senior executives will never understand information risk, but this is not entirely correct. They may not understand the technicalities of information security, but risk is something they will definitely understand, so the streetwise information risk management programme manager will ensure that all reporting is couched in terms of risk to the organisation and the business benefits to be gained by avoiding, transferring, reducing or accepting it.

BUSINESS CASES

Business cases are a standard vehicle for demonstrating a genuine need to carry out some form of activity that will require senior management approval. They are generally used under circumstances in which a significant financial spend is proposed, and, in the case of an information risk management programme, will most frequently be brought into play in gaining approval to carry out risk reduction or modification.

In some situations, the business case might present senior management with a clear and simple 'yes or no' decision, whilst others might involve a number of options with a recommendation for a specific approach that, in the view of the information risk management programme, represents the most appropriate solution, combined with good value for money. In the case of the latter, the senior management team will be required to choose their favourite option, and the contents of the business case will heavily influence this choice.

It follows, therefore, that the business case should be as comprehensive and compelling as possible, so that senior management's decision-making process is made as simple as possible, and that they make a fully informed choice.

There is no generic set format for a business case. Some organisations have their own template, whereas others allow a free format of presentation. In this section, we suggest some of the essential components of the business case and describe how best to present it.

Most people will be familiar with the name of Robert Maxwell who ran a vast publishing business empire that included newspapers like *The New York Times*, *The Daily Mirror*, *The Scottish Daily Record* and *The European*. Whatever his faults, he adopted a very simple approach to business cases. He relied on his senior management team to pull together the best advice and to present this to him in as short a time as possible.

When it came to receiving his formal approval, a single sheet of A4 was all he needed to read, written in a 14-point Courier typeface, with 1.5 line spacing, and a signature line near the bottom of the page followed by the words 'Approved. R Maxwell, Chairman'. Supporting information was always stapled behind this, but he rarely needed to study it.

Most senior executives do not have the time to read huge amounts of detail, and since information security is not usually their strongest point, might find it difficult to follow. What they do need are clear, concise facts, the costs, the benefits to be gained and, if necessary, the downsides of not choosing the recommended option.

It is suggested that a business case document should contain the following sections:

- an introductory executive summary – preferably on a single page;
- the benefits to the organisation of undertaking the work;
- a synopsis of the goals and objectives and the main risks threatening the information assets, together with the likely impacts or consequences faced by the organisation if the threats were to occur;
- a synopsis of the proposed solution, together with reasoning as to how and why this would eliminate the risk or reduce it to a level acceptable to the organisation, and the timescales for doing so;
- a financial breakdown, showing both capital and operating expenditure required over a three to five year period, with resources for premises, equipment and people clearly identified;
- a high-level project overview, including critical success factors;
- an implementation plan including resources required, a timeline and key milestones.

Many organisations prefer a personal briefing as well as a business case document, in which case a slide presentation – probably no more than ten slides – should be prepared and delivered by a programme representative who feels comfortable presenting to very senior managers, and who can also answer penetrating questions without the need to refer to detailed notes.

Whichever approach is taken, the person presenting the business case would be well advised to socialise the business case beforehand with as many members of the approving committee as possible, so that it is approved 'on the nod'. This approach has another advantage, in that many of the questions that might be asked during a presentation will either be known or answered beforehand, and any last-minute changes to the business case that will assist in gaining approval can be included.

RISK TREATMENT DECISION-MAKING

The decision-making process for risk treatment follows a logical path. It begins with identifying the strategic option or options that the organisation should take – risk avoidance or termination; risk transfer or sharing; risk reduction or modification; risk acceptance or tolerance – and this part of the process will have been taken care of during risk evaluation, the final stage of risk assessment.

The next step for each of the chosen strategic approaches is to identify the tactical options. These will depend completely on the strategic approaches, but will be as follows:

- Risk avoidance or termination presents both preventative and detective options, but these are used together, since the preventative course of action will require ongoing (detective) monitoring to ensure that further action is taken if something changes.

- Risk transfer or sharing has both directive and detective options and again these are used together, since any shared risk also requires ongoing monitoring to ensure that it is working as expected.

- Risk reduction or modification is the most complex, as it can involve directive, detective, preventative and corrective actions, again with ongoing monitoring.

- Finally, risk acceptance of tolerance follows the detective approach with ongoing monitoring, and it is very important to repeat that no risk, no matter how trivial it might appear, should ever be ignored.

Having identified the tactical risk treatment options, the final stage is to identify the operational options:

- Risk avoidance utilises both detective and preventative controls. The preventative controls will almost always be physical or technical, and the detective controls will always be procedural.

- Risk transfer's detective controls will usually be procedural (in the case of insurance, for example), or may be both technical and procedural in the example of outsourcing operations to a Cloud service provider.

- Risk reduction uses all three types of operational control. Preventative controls can be either physical (e.g. security barriers) or technical (e.g. firewalls). Corrective controls can be physical, technical (e.g. ensuring that bug fixes are applied to software), or procedural. Directive controls are instructive, and therefore always procedural, and include policies, processes and works instructions. Detective controls can be physical (e.g. closed-circuit TV systems), technical (e.g. intrusion detection software) or procedural (e.g. system activity monitoring).

- Finally, risk acceptance requires just detective procedural controls to provide ongoing monitoring of threats to ensure that the level of risk has not changed.

RISK TREATMENT PLANNING AND IMPLEMENTATION

It is quite conceivable that many of the risks requiring treatment as part of the information risk management programme can undergo this as an integral part of the programme. However, some risks might require extensive (or expensive) treatment, and as such may need to be treated as a project or programme of work in their own right. However, although the implementation may be carried out under a separate project or programme, progress reporting of the implementation should remain part of the original information risk management programme so that the audit trail is complete. Such a project requires the setting of goals, objectives, scope and milestones, which, given the controls recommended and agreed earlier in the information risk management programme, should be relatively straightforward to define.

The risk treatment plan should commence with the production of a prioritised list of risks for treatment, which includes realistic estimates of the length of time these might take to achieve, the approximate cost of the treatment and the resources required (including the name of the responsible person) of doing so. By totalling the number of completed risk treatments and the running costs, additional information can be reported to senior management.

Regardless of whether the project is to be managed from within or outside the main information risk management programme, resources, especially people and funding, must have been agreed and committed by the organisation. This will include a suitably-qualified project manager, who may be a different entity from the information risk management programme manager, particularly if the project is significant in its scope; for example, if the agreed control is for the provision of an entire backup data centre with high-availability standby systems, this would be a major project in its own right, and would certainly require at least one dedicated project manager, if not several. However, even if the remedial work to implement the agreed controls is relatively minor, each individual control should be considered as a task within an overall project, so that it can have resources assigned to it and be tracked to completion and sign-off.

BUSINESS CONTINUITY AND DISASTER RECOVERY

Occasionally, the controls recommended may be very wide-ranging, such as the need for business continuity management (BCM) arrangements, which are specialist subject areas in their own right. However, it is worth providing a brief description of both approaches.

Business continuity

The concept of BC became better known in 2006 with the introduction of the first full Standard, BS 25999-1 *Code of Practice*, and BS 25999-2 *Specification* in 2007. Prior to that, there had only ever been a publicly available specification, PAS 56, published in 2003 and developed from an early Business Continuity Institute *Good Practice Guidelines* document.

The two BS 25999 Standards were superseded in 2012 by the international Standard, ISO 22301:2012 *Societal security – BCM systems – Requirements*.

We have defined BC in our Glossary of Terms as 'the capability of the organisation to continue delivery of products and services at acceptable pre-defined levels following a disruptive incident' (ISO 22301:2012).

BC applies to a number of key areas within an organisation, and so is considered to be a holistic approach to risk management. It includes:

- the people employed by the organisation, together with its contractors;
- the organisation's premises, whether these are offices, factories, warehouses or other types of building;
- the organisation's processes and procedures;
- the technology that supports the organisation's activities;
- the organisation's information in both physical and electronic forms;
- the organisation's supply chain;
- any other stakeholders that have an interest in the organisation;
- the organisation's responsibilities in the event of civil emergencies.

At first sight, it would appear that information is just one of these areas, but it actually cuts across all of the remainder, and hence the principles explored in information risk management are fundamental to the discipline of BCM.

The Business Continuity Institute Good Practice Guidelines 2013

Founded in 1994, the Business Continuity Institute (BCI) has always been at the forefront of business continuity standards development, and was instrumental in the first UK specification, PAS 56, published in 2003. Its members have subsequently taken a leading role in the later development of BS 25999 in 2006/7 and ISO 22301 in 2012.

Over the years, the Institute has developed a set of good practice guidelines (GPGs) that define the generic approach to BCM in six distinct stages, or so-called Professional Practices (PPs):

- **PP1 Policy and Programme Management.** This is the beginning of the overall BCM lifecycle, and defines the organisation's policy for business continuity – how it will be implemented, managed and tested.

- **PP2 Embedding Business Continuity.** It is important that the culture of BCM is embedded into day-to-day operations within an organisation.

- **PP3 Analysis.** In earlier versions of the *Good Practice Guidelines*, this was known as Understanding the Organisation, and assesses the organisation's overall objectives, how it functions and the internal and external context within which it operates. It includes the risk assessment process of risk management.

- **PP4 Design.** Formerly known as Determining Business Continuity Strategy, this area recommends suitable approaches (both strategic and tactical) to recover from disruptive events and to provide continuity of operations.

- **PP5 Implementation.** This area was previously known as Determining and Implementing a BCM Response, and carries out the recommended and agreed approaches through the development of business continuity plans. Together with Design, this area aligns with the risk treatment portion of risk management.

- **PP6 Validation.** Validation was originally referred to as Exercising, Maintaining and Reviewing, and deals with the validation of business continuity plans through tests and exercises to ensure that they are fit for purpose and would be effective in disruptive situations.

PPs 1 and 2 are described as management practices, whereas PPs 3 to 6 are described as technical practices. The Business Continuity Institute's lifecycle diagram illustrates this graphically in Figure 8.1.

Figure 8.1 The BCI lifecycle

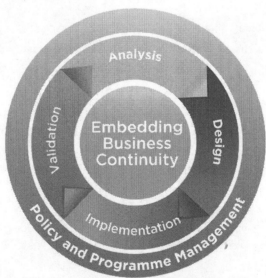

Source: Professional Practice descriptions and the BCI Lifecycle diagram are used with the kind permission of The Business Continuity Institute.

These are by no means mandatory requirements, but most BC practitioners – and not only in the UK – will follow them, since they provide considerable assistance when an organisation wishes to become compliant with the Standard and to achieve accreditation against it.

The plans produced will include:

- incident management (IM) plans, which deal with the immediate aftermath of business-disrupting incidents, and which can include information security incidents as well as civil emergencies, strikes and pandemics;
- business continuity (BC) plans, which take the process following IM through recovery to a normal or near-normal state;
- disaster recovery (DR) plans, which deal mainly with restoring the capability of ICT systems;
- business resumption (BR) plans, which are the final stage of recovering from incidents, and which take operations back to the same state as they were in prior to the incident.

Although BC itself is generally thought of as being a form of risk reduction or modification, a BC programme of work may well make use of all forms of strategic, tactical and operational controls in order to achieve its objectives.

BC introduces some terminology that is not generally used in information risk management. However, when implementing a BC strategy as part of the treatment process for an information risk management programme, it is worthwhile being aware of them:

- **recovery point objective (RPO).** The point to which information used by an activity must be restored to enable the activity to operate on resumption;
- **recovery time objective (RTO).** The period of time following an incident within which products, services or activities must be resumed, or resources must be recovered;
- **maximum acceptable outage (MAO).** The time it would take for adverse impacts – which might arise as a result of not providing a product/service or performing an activity – to become unacceptable;
- **maximum tolerable data loss (MTDL).** The maximum loss of information (electronic and other data) which an organisation can tolerate. The age of the data could make operational recovery impossible or the value of the lost data is so substantial as to put business viability at risk;
- **maximum tolerable period of disruption (MTPD).** The time it would take for adverse impacts – which might arise as a result of not providing a product/ service or performing an activity – to become unacceptable;
- **minimum business continuity objective (MBCO).** The minimum level of services and/or products that is acceptable to the organisation to achieve its business objectives during a disruption.

Figure 8.2 illustrates the BC incident timeline.

Figure 8.2 The generic business continuity incident timeline

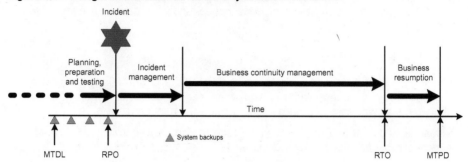

Once IM, BCM, DR and BR plans have been developed, they must be tested in order to prove their fitness for purpose. Various types of test may be undertaken:

- communications tests, in which the contact procedures are tested to ensure that members of the various teams responsible for managing the situation can be contacted and instructed to attend the crisis management centre;

- desktop read-throughs, in which the plans are scrutinised by all members of the various response and recovery teams in order to verify that all necessary activities have been identified, that they are in the correct order and that all interdependencies have been considered;

- scenario-based exercises, in which the BC manager develops an imaginary or real-world event-based scenario for the response and recovery teams to work through as if it were an actual event. Lessons learnt from this type of exercise will often refine the plans as gaps and overlaps are identified;

- full-scale exercises, again, usually scenario-based, in which many or all of the organisation's staff are involved to some extent in order to verify that the plans do actually work in situations as close as possible to real-world events. Such exercises will disrupt the organisation's business activities, and will only be performed under exceptional circumstances.

BC is invariably conducted as a separate programme of work from that of information risk management, since it has much wider implications for the organisation, especially in terms of the resources required to operate the programme and to exercise the plans.

Disaster recovery

DR is a specialised subset of BC, and is generally used to refer to the arrangements put in place to provide backup or recovery computing facilities, although it can refer to other forms of technical processing. In our Glossary of Terms, we describe DR as 'A coordinated activity to enable the recovery of ICT systems and networks due to a disruption'.

Some organisations make use of system hardware used normally for testing purposes to provide DR, sometimes on a one-for-one basis, so that the standby hardware is identical to the system being replicated, and sometimes on a one-to-many basis, where one system can be used to provide DR for a number of systems. The overall structure for disaster recovery is illustrated in Figure 8.3 below.

Figure 8.3 Overall structure for disaster recovery

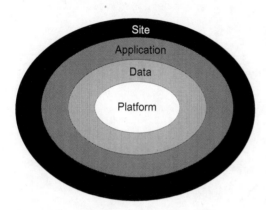

Site – Site recovery; site data centre failover

Application – Application failover/load balancing; redundant systems

Data – Storage area networks; network-attached storage; direct-attached storage; data backup and restore

Platform – Rapid equipment replacement; high availability systems

Platform disaster recovery

Platform DR generally involves the use of one or more of the following types of facility:

Cold standby platforms. These consist of bare computer systems and associated communications equipment. They may have an operating system loaded, but little else. The organisation or its outsourced DR partner will be responsible for loading any applications software required in order to operate the system in the same way as the one it is replicating. In addition, all data must be restored from backup media, and the organisation will need to take into account any patches or software updates that have been issued.

Because these systems are very basic, they represent the lowest cost to an organisation, but take the longest amount of time to bring up to full operation.

Warm standby platforms. Warm standby systems invariably have their operating system and key applications loaded, and may have backed-up data loaded as well. However, unless the system has been maintained in a fully 'ready' state, the organisation will need to take into account any patches or software updates that have been issued since the system was originally configured. Data will have to be brought fully up to date by restoring from the most recent backups.

Warm standby systems are more expensive to provide than cold standby systems, but can normally be brought into service much more quickly.

Hot standby/high-availability platforms. At the top end of the DR range there are hot standby or high-availability platforms, which are always maintained in a fully ready state from the point of view of operating systems and application software. Data will also be fully up to date, since the system being replicated will copy across all data onto the standby system.

These vary in type and cost, as can be seen from Figure 8.4. Availability is measured in 'nines', with five nines, i.e. 99.999%, availability being the highest, which allows for five minutes' downtime in any twelve-month period. Unsurprisingly, higher availability comes with a greatly increased cost, and each 'nine' added would probably increase the cost tenfold.

Figure 8.4 Cost versus availability

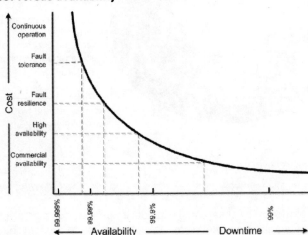

In cases where two systems operate jointly to deliver the service, data is copied between the live and the standby system in one of two ways:

- asynchronous replication, in which each block of data is sent from the live system to the standby system, receipt is confirmed, but the live system continues to process data in the meantime;

- synchronous replication, in which each block of data is sent from the live system to the standby system, but the live system waits before continuing to process data until receipt is confirmed.

Synchronous replication is slightly slower than asynchronous replication, but has greater reliability since no data can be lost at the point of switchover. The distance between the live and standby locations cannot currently be greater than around 200 km, and typically uses a direct fibre optic link, which guarantees capacity as well as reliability.

High-availability systems are by far the most costly to operate, but for organisations such as banks, large online retail organisations, airlines and the like, failure of service and possible loss of information is simply not an option.

In conjunction with platform DR, organisations should take into account four key areas:

- Resilient power, in which uninterruptible power supplies (UPSs) ensure that power is always available to the platforms. UPS systems feed power from the incoming mains supply during normal operation, and batteries take over and generate the appropriate levels of power through static inverters if and when the incoming supply fails. In order to make the power supplies completely resilient, standby generation can also be used, but resilience of fuel supplies for these must then be taken into account.

- Cooling systems are also highly necessary to take away excess heat and allow the systems to operate at a comfortable temperature. It is common practice to allow at least one more cooling system than is necessary to maintain a constant temperature, and this is referred to as N+1.

  Since system hardware can run at temperatures higher than staff would find comfortable, some organisations run the equipment rooms of their data centres slightly warmer, which can reduce cooling costs without a detrimental effect on the systems.

- Systems and service monitoring is always required so that remedial action can be taken as soon as there is a failure in any part of the service being provided. In larger organisations, the internal and external data networks are usually monitored in addition to platforms and services.

- Vendor support is the final key requirement for all operations of this kind, simply because the systems vendor organisations can often supply additional or replacement platforms either at the data centre itself, or increasingly through Cloud services.

Data resilience

Although data storage has moved on considerably in recent years, magnetic media of one kind or another remains the most cost-effective technology, although it is rarely the fastest. There are several commonly used methods of providing resilient data storage:

- **redundant array of inexpensive disks (RAID)**, which uses several different technologies to achieve various levels of resilience, including error correction, striping and mirroring, some of which will permit a faulty disk drive to be exchanged without loss of any data whatsoever. There are currently around 12 different levels of RAID, and different operating systems (e.g. Unix, Linux, MAC OS X and Microsoft Windows support slightly different combinations of RAID level). In general, the RAID systems that use more disk drives provide greater resilience, but there are advantages and disadvantages of all types in terms of ease of implementation, cost, resilience and performance;

- **direct attached storage (DAS)**, in which RAID arrays are connected directly to a system using a standard RAID controller. DAS is less resilient than other methods, in that access must always be via the system and controller to which it is connected, which presents a potential single point of failure;

- **network attached storage (NAS)**, unlike DAS storage, does not rely on a separate system for connection but instead uses its own proprietary operating system and connects directly to a network. This means that it can be accessed in a more flexible manner, making deployment much more straightforward. The ongoing increase of LAN speeds makes NAS a very attractive option. NAS storage also has the advantage of being able to operate at block level as well as at file level, making it independent of the host operating system;

- **storage area networks (SAN)** make use of highly resilient fibre optic links between the host systems and their storage arrays, which are also designed to be highly resilient. Operating completely at the block level, they are completely independent of the host operating system.

Application resilience

We are all used to experiencing applications on a home or office computer, and these occasionally fail, but usually impact only the computer user. At a corporate level, application failures will affect many users, and those that provide service for online use (for example, online banking applications) can affect very large numbers of people if they fail. For this reason, application resilience is key to such services, and can be delivered in one of three ways:

- Clustered file systems distribute the file system across multiple systems or nodes, each of which holds part of the overall file system, but appears to the end user as a single system. They provide a very high throughput, but at high cost of deployment and management.

- Application clusters, which are similar to clustered file systems, but which distribute just the application software across multiple systems, provide increased performance and availability. The host computer sees the application as a single resource, which requires the use of a so-called 'heartbeat' between all the systems in the cluster so that a node that has failed can be flagged as such and its resources transferred across the remaining online nodes. Application clusters are quite complex to deploy.

- Computer cluster services include two key options. The first is load balancing, in which the network traffic is distributed as evenly as possible across multiple web servers which all share a single IP address, and the load balancing software uses a rule-set to decide which server should receive the next request. The second is failover cluster services, which has two sub-options. In the first option, all nodes in a cluster have access to shared resources (such as DAS, NAS or SAN), and a heartbeat similar to that used in application clusters is used to assist in the control of access to nodes. This is sometimes referred to as the 'share everything' approach. In the second option, known as 'share nothing', only one node in a cluster has access to the resources at any one time.

Disaster recovery failover testing

The testing of DR plans generally follows one of two paths:

- 'fire drills', which normally refer to the testing of DR plans in which the process of bringing the standby systems into full readiness is tested, but stops short of an actual switchover from live to standby systems since, depending on the type of standby system implemented, this might be disruptive to the organisation's business;

- full switchover tests, in which not only are the standby systems brought into a state of full readiness, but also a switchover from live to standby systems is performed and the performance of the new system status is verified as being at an acceptable level.

Again, depending on the type of standby system implemented, a full switchover test might be disruptive, but it is the only way in which the organisation can be completely certain that its DR arrangements are fully working. However, if the standby system has been correctly implemented, everything should failover without interruption.

9 COMMUNICATION, CONSULTATION, MONITORING AND REVIEW

Before we examine the requirements for communication, consultation, monitoring and review within an information risk management programme, let us take a few moments to examine the kinds of skills an information risk programme manager will require. These include:

- **Business skills.** A sound knowledge of the organisation's business is essential when commencing an impact assessment. This will include not only an understanding of the key activities, products and services, but also how the organisation goes about its business including areas such as sales and marketing, order processing and fulfilment, procurement, manufacturing, finance and human resources.

- **Technical skills.** Although the person conducting the impact assessment will be unlikely to have a detailed technical knowledge of all the processes involved, this is not necessarily a bad thing. An appreciation of technical issues is, however, a distinct advantage as it permits one to ask 'obvious' questions, the answers to which can occasionally highlight a potential problem.

- **Interviewing skills.** Interviewing skills can be learnt, but if this option is not open, then the interviewer should take a few basic rules into account. First, he or she should explain the purpose of the discussion clearly, and verify that the interviewee has understood. Second, it is essential to have a prepared list of questions.

  Often, one question will trigger another that was not on the list, so a degree of flexibility is also required. The interviewer should always listen more then he or she speaks as the objective is for the interviewer to discover information and for the interviewee to provide it.

  Interviews should not take more than an hour or so as the interviewee may provide less valuable information if the process is lengthy, and the interviewer will have difficulty in absorbing sufficient information. If time runs out, the interviewer should conclude the discussion, write up the notes and continue at a later date. This also allows the interviewee to review the output and confirm the earlier discussion.

- **Analytical skills.** Analysis of the output from interviews is required in order to ensure that all areas of the organisation have been covered and that the findings are also consistent across the whole organisation.

- **Presentation skills.** Presentation skills can also be learnt. Presentation of the results of the impact assessments may well be to a senior management team who will look critically at the resulting requests and recommendations for work to be carried out and resources (including finance) to be made available for later risk treatment. For this reason, the final presentation must be clear, succinct and accurate.

- **Interpersonal skills.** The skills we have already described are necessary in order for the information risk management programme manager to undertake the role, but more important than all of these are the interpersonal skills on which all the others depend.

Interpersonal skills include:

- verbal skills, which are all about what we say to other people and the way in which we say it;
- non-verbal skills include what both we and other people do not say, but do indicate in gestures and body language;
- listening skills are the way in which we interpret both the verbal and non-verbal information given by others;
- negotiation skills are the way in which we work with other people to agree a mutually acceptable outcome;
- problem solving skills are where we work with other people to identify and define problems, explore possible solutions and make recommendations;
- decision-making skills are where we explore and analyse multiple options to make sound decisions;
- assertiveness skills include communicating our values, ideas, beliefs, opinions, needs and wants, but without aggressiveness.

COMMUNICATION

One of the most important components of any information risk management programme is that of communication. As with any project or programme, nothing useful will ever be delivered unless those involved communicate effectively with one another.

An experienced programme manager will be aware of the possibility of a 'lone wolf' member of the team who will be tempted to work independently of everyone else, and who may not be willing to share information or progress with others or, occasionally, to take on board what others have already done. This will invariably lead to duplication of effort and mistakes being made as assessments, analyses and evaluations are carried out, recommendations made and decisions implemented all in complete isolation and without taking full account of the larger picture.

Communication is also a two-way process. Information provided must be acknowledged, and information requested must be delivered. However, bottlenecks can and will occur, especially in larger organisations and in those with relatively rigid hierarchical management chains.

It is not uncommon for the progress of the message through the management chain to stop at some point – especially if there is bad news to be told – or for information to be either diluted or embellished – especially if the news could jeopardise someone's career or if a particular pet project is under threat.

The means and route of communication should have been agreed in the early stages of the programme, and it is suggested that a simple reporting format is always the best, since it presents the information in a way in which all levels of management can understand without the need for large quantities of detailed information. These may mean little to a senior manager or director, but if further information is required, this can either be attached if the need has been anticipated, or can be requested at the time.

One of the greatest risks over and above those we are considering in an information risk management programme is that of miscommunication. Verbal reports should really be considered as an informal briefing, although they are frequently taken as being both formal and factual; in response to an innocent 'How's it going?' question, the unwary information risk management programme manager might answer 'It's going well', and this could suddenly turn into a boardroom view that there are no issues.

Verbal communication is something to be extremely wary of providing unless written or graphical notes can back it up. Also, the potential audience can make a great deal of difference – briefing an internal audience might include concerns regarding particular information sets or projects, but it might well be wholly inappropriate to allow these to become known to external stakeholders. In such circumstances, it is always best to follow up even the most brief enquiry with a quick email that expands on this, so that the enquirer's expectations are met, and there is no doubt left as to what 'It's going well' actually means.

A common means of reporting is the so-called 'traffic light' method, in which any individual risk's status can be expressed as:

- Green. Green risk status indicates that the risk has been successfully treated and is now at or below the level deemed acceptable by the organisation's risk appetite.

- Amber. Risks reported as Amber are currently in the process of being treated or are acceptable at that level, and it is the view of the information risk management programme manager that treatment will ultimately be successful.

- Red. Reporting a risk as Red indicates that the risk has not yet been treated; the risk is potentially untreatable; treatment has been unsuccessful and the residual risk is above the level deemed acceptable by the organisation's risk appetite; or that the organisation has agreed to accept the risk at that level.

It is also possible to show in a separate column whether or not treatment of the risk is on schedule, for example:

- Green status could represent the view that treatment was either on or ahead of schedule.

- Amber might be interpreted to mean that the risk was in danger of falling behind schedule, especially if activities were dependent upon the treatment of another risk that was already behind schedule.

- Red would mean that treatment of a risk was behind schedule.

Further, the overall status of the information risk management programme can be summarised by representing the number of outstanding risks in any risk category in a similar way, and by agreeing in advance the percentage of risks that fall into each of the three categories, for example:

- Green. Up to 35% of individual risks at Red status.

- Amber. 35% to 65% of individual risks at Red status.

- Red. More than 65% of individual risks at Red status.

Whatever the method chosen to report the progress or status of an information risk management programme, the content should ensure that it is jargon-free, since some of the readership may either be completely unfamiliar with this, or may interpret its meaning differently from that intended.

The report should ensure that the reader is fully informed about the topic, using clear and concise language and providing a balanced interpretation of the information risk management programme status, since to be too over-or under-optimistic can result in problems further down the line. Where possible, the report must supply the reader with all the answers they might reasonable have regarding the topic. It is, of course, impossible to anticipate all the questions that might arise, but the information risk management programme manager should be able to anticipate the most likely questions and ensure that answers to those not anticipated are included in subsequent reports.

In cases where a decision will be required as a direct result of submitting the report, the wording should leave the reader in no doubt that a firm decision is required, what the choices are (if any), the date by which a decision is required and what the next steps will be following the decision.

If presentation of the report is to be in the form of slides, then the information risk management programme manager should ensure that the presentation format is clear and free of over-ornate typefaces and graphics, so that the format does not dilute the message.

Senior managers, and boards of directors especially, invariably have a limited amount of time in which to view the presentation, so brevity is essential. The need for decisions and the next steps should always be summarised on the final presentation slide.

CONSULTATION

Consultation is simply another form of communication, but one in which questions are asked and answers given as opposed to information provided on a routine basis or when requested.

Consultation begins right at the start of the information risk management programme. The programme manager must consult at all levels both within and outside the organisation in order to:

- understand the goals, scope and objectives of the programme;
- identify the key roles and responsibilities needed to undertake the programme;
- understand how governance of the programme will by managed;
- understand the internal and external contexts within which the organisation operates;
- understand the organisation's risk appetite for various types and classes of risk;
- identify what risk treatment criteria it wishes to set for risk avoidance or termination; risk transfer or sharing; risk reduction or modification; risk acceptance or tolerance;
- identify the threshold for costs of risk treatment, above which a business case will be required.

That done, the programme manager can begin to:

- plan the programme;
- make contact with the most appropriate people or groups within and outside the organisation;
- identify the organisation's information assets and agree their owners;
- obtain impact or consequence information from them;
- obtain threat and vulnerability information.

Much if not all of this information will originate from individual directors, managers and specialist staff within the organisation, although some may have to be obtained from external sources such as suppliers, consultants and security-related organisations.

The consultation process itself will require similar skills to those described in Chapter 4.

RISK REVIEWS AND MONITORING

If we think back to the PDCA cycle we discussed in Chapter 2, we can see that the Check part of the cycle covers the requirement for monitor and review. This is an important part of the information risk management programme, since it will enable us to verify that treatment has been carried out correctly and that it has been successful. It enables us to:

- verify that the controls we have put in place have been effective, both in cost and functionality;
- identify those areas where controls have been less successful, and take remedial action to resolve these;

- identify new risks, and take them through the risk management process;
- identify areas where the vulnerabilities have increased or decreased;
- identify areas where the likelihood of risks occurring have increased or decreased;
- consider new information assets that have been added to the organisation's portfolio;
- revise impact assessments for information assets whose value to the organisation has increased or decreased due to changing business circumstances;
- take account of information security incidents that have resulted in harm to the organisation's information assets;
- consider the use of other methodologies as a means of conducting the information risk management programme;
- be mindful that some information assets exhibit considerable interdependence and therefore, if one risk changes, other dependent risks will also change.

Risk reviews

There may be some temptation to assume that, once a risk has been treated, its treatment has been completely successful and we can forget about it for the time being since no further treatment would appear to be required. This is a very bad idea because, at this stage, we do not know for certain either that the risk has truly been treated successfully, or that the treatment has not introduced additional risks.

The first stage of the risk review commences with a revisit of the original risk assessment process to verify that either the impact or the likelihood has been reduced and to calculate a revised risk level. If this calculation indicates that the hoped-for level of risk has actually been attained and any residual risk is within the organisation's risk appetite, then the treatment can be considered to have been completely successful. If, however, the level of risk attained has not achieved this, but has been reduced below that of the organisation's risk appetite, treatment can be considered to have been partially successful and a decision can be made as to whether or not to introduce additional controls in an attempt to reduce the level of risk still further. If it transpires that the resulting level of risk remains above that of the organisation's risk appetite, then treatment will have been unsuccessful, and a complete re-assessment of possible controls will be required. All of this must then be recorded in the risk register to ensure that there is a sound audit trail.

The second stage of the risk review involves an examination of whether or not the original risk treatment introduced any additional risks, or whether it has had an impact on other risks that we have been treating and has either raised or reduced the level of risk in them. The overall number of risks treated as part of the information risk management programme may be too many to examine in one review, and it may be more convenient either to review a proportion of the risks in several stages, or to review only those risks that were identified as being high or very high, so that the most critical risks are reviewed.

Risk reviews are best conducted as a group or team activity, since, although an individual manager may have all the requisite skills to carry out the work, a wider perspective can result in more accurate reviews and assessments.

Risk monitoring

Risk monitoring takes a slightly different approach from risk review. Whereas risk review occurs immediately or soon after risk treatment, risk monitoring is an ongoing process that verifies the risk status at regular intervals.

It is also important to monitor the information risk management programme and activities themselves in order to ensure that other factors that have changed are taken into account, such as the organisation's:

- business strategy and direction;
- levels of risk tolerance and risk appetite;
- impact, risk evaluation and risk acceptance criteria;
- resources available to engage in the information risk management programme;
- approach to the controls it chooses when assessing treating risks;
- the internal or external context in which the organisation finds itself, including the competitive context where this is appropriate and the legal and regulatory context.

The periodic basis for risk monitoring should be based on two sets of criteria:

- First, the higher the level of residual risk, the more frequent the monitoring should be – clearly, higher level risks being monitored more frequently than lower-level ones.
- Second, for those risks whose threat level does not change quickly – for example, legal and regulatory changes – the risk monitoring may be less frequent, whereas for those risks whose threat level changes more frequently – for example, viruses and software vulnerabilities – the monitoring should be much more frequent.

There will often be a temptation to only monitor the risks annually. Unless they exhibit either a very slow-changing threat level, or the residual risk is very low, this should be avoided, since many attributes of the organisation and its internal and external contexts may have changed over 12 months, and some old or new risks could easily be overlooked. As with risk reviews, all risk monitoring output should be recorded in the risk register.

10 THE CESG IA CERTIFICATION SCHEME

THE CESG IA CERTIFICATION SCHEME

Anyone who wishes to work in the information security environment, either within a government organisation or as a contractor to one, must be accredited to do so regardless of any additional security clearances that may be required.

The scheme, known as CLAS (CESG Listed Advisor Scheme) requires that to join CLAS, applicants must:

- have IA certification in any role, at any responsibility level;
- be able to hold and retain a Security Clearance;
- have sponsorship of a UK Limited Company;
- have some experience of information risk management in the public sector.

The certification referred to is known as the CESG Certified Professional (CCP) scheme, and is not merely a qualification, but a full certification awarded to individuals who are able to demonstrate an application of their skills, knowledge and expertise to one of three approved certification bodies.

The CESG website, http://www.cesg.gov.uk/AwarenessTraining/certified-professionals/Pages/index.aspx, contains comprehensive details of the scheme, which encompasses seven different role areas:

- Accreditor. Accreditors provide impartial assessment of risks to which an information system may be exposed, and accredit such systems on behalf of the organisation's senior management.
- IA Auditor. Auditors assess compliance with security objectives, policies, standards and processes.
- IA Architect. Security architects develop and review system architectures so that they fit the business requirements for security, mitigate risks and conform to security policies, and balance information risk against the cost of controls.
- Security and Information Risk Advisor (SIRA). The SIRA's role is to provide business driven advice on security and information risk that is consistent with government policy, standards and guidance.

- Information Technology Security Officer (ITSO). The ITSO's role is to provide governance of IT security.

- Communications Security Officer (COMSO). The COMSO's role is to ensure compliance with the government communications security and cryptography requirements.

- Penetration tester.

Each role may be assessed at one of three levels except for the penetration tester, which has four levels and includes a principal level. Otherwise, they are:

- practitioner;

- senior practitioner;

- lead practitioner.

Two different sets of skills, knowledge and expertise are assessed:

- The SFIA levels of responsibility for autonomy, influence, complexity and business skills. Many of the practitioner, senior practitioner and lead practitioner roles align with SFIA levels 2, 4 and 6. More detail is available from http://www.sfia-online.org and is also provided in the Skills Framework for the Information Age section of this chapter.

- The IISP (Institute of Information Security Professionals) skills matrix for information security technical skills, more information on which is provided at: https://www.iisp.org/imis15/iisp/About_Us/Our_Skills_Framework/iisp/About_Us/Our_Skills_Framework.aspx?hkey=6a996e64-4c90-4892-bb7e-b3d6e5dff3d5 and in The IISP Skills Framework section of this chapter.

Each of the three levels for each of the six roles is described in greater detail in 'Certification for IA professionals, Issue 4.0, March 2014', available from CESG at: http://www.cesg.gov.uk/publications/Documents/cesg_certification_for_ia_professionals.pdf

In the main body of the document, each role has a brief role purpose description and a statement of responsibilities, followed by a 'headline' statement, which outlines the key responsibilities of the role for each of the three practitioner levels. This is followed by a table listing the indicative IISP skill levels for the three role levels.

The penetration tester's role is further described in greater detail, since very particular knowledge areas and skills are involved, and this role has its own Appendix, which places additional requirements on senior and principal penetration testers in the following areas:

- engagement, legislation and risk;

- core technical knowledge;

- information gathering;

- networking;
- microsoft Windows security assessment;
- UNIX security assessment;
- databases;
- web technologies;
- physical access and security;
- web application security assessment (as an area of specialism).

The Annexes of the document contain a very detailed description of the IISP skill definitions. Each skill area begins with a statement of the IISP Principle, followed by the knowledge requirements for that skill area. Following on from this, each skill subset (e.g. Governance under Information Security Management) is described in terms of IISP example skills and as a GESG supplementation of the attainment expected for each of the four skill levels.

Certification is carried out by any one of three organisations – The APM Group, BCS, and the Chartered Institute for IT together with a consortium of the IISP, CREST and the Royal Holloway University of London. The three organisations operate slightly different schemes with different costs, and prospective candidates are recommended to view the various options on the main CCP page at: http://www.cesg.gov.uk/awarenesstraining/certified-professionals/Pages/Certification-Bodies.aspx

In addition to completing an application form that itemises and describes their SFIA and IISP skill sets, candidates are strongly advised to have gained a thorough understanding of the following documents, the first of which is summarised in Chapter 11:

- HMG Security Policy Framework;
- HMG IA Standard Numbers 1 and 2 – Information Risk Management;
- HMG IA Standard Numbers 1 and 2 – Supplement Technical Risk Assessment and Risk Treatment;
- Good Practice Guide No. 19 – Managing Accreditation – Governance, Structure and Culture;
- Good Practice Guide No.47 – information Risk Management.

The Security Policy Framework is available for download at: https://www.gov.uk/government/publications/security-policy-framework

The remaining documents must be requested directly from CESG. However, please note that prior to publication, CESG advised the author that they plan to retire IA Standard Numbers 1 and 2, but have not indicated the likely timescales.

IA, CESG, B2h
Hubble Road
Cheltenham
Gloucestershire
GL51 0EX

Tel: +44 (0) 1242 709141
Fax: +44 (0) 1242 709193
Email: enquiries@cesg.gsi.gov.uk

SKILLS FRAMEWORK FOR THE INFORMATION AGE (SFIA)

Whilst many of the skills required by information risk management practitioners are technical in nature, there are just as many professional skills required of them. Established in 2003, the Skills Framework for the Information Age (SFIA) was designed as a system aimed at IT professionals to match their skills against business requirements, and it represents those business-related skills expected of a practitioner who applies to join the CESG Listed Advisor Scheme (CLAS).

SFIA skills make a clearly identifiable differentiation between professional and technical skills, and it is the professional side that is used within the CLAS scheme. The SFIA framework invites applicants to demonstrate their capability in four key business-related competences.

Autonomy

Whilst not actually a competence in its own right, but demonstrating a degree of professional freedom, autonomy examines individuals' levels of responsibility and authority within an organisation. It defines the degree to which individuals are accountable to higher levels of management; their limits of delegation, decision-making and direction setting; whether they can act with independence or with more detailed reference to others; and the circumstances under which they need to escalate queries or problems.

An individual's degree of autonomy will dictate the extent to which they can develop, direct and implement policies and standards within an organisation; generate processes and procedures; set organisational objectives; and make decisions.

Influence

The ability of individuals to demonstrate influence within an organisation will be heavily dependent upon the degree of autonomy they are permitted within their role. Influence, however, is much more of a competence in that individuals need to understand whom they should influence, and just as importantly when to do so. The extent of individuals' influence, both above and below them within an organisation, is often referred to as the sphere of influence, but this can also be taken to mean the business constraints within which they operate, such as technical, financial or organisational.

Additionally, individuals may influence strategy and decision-making within an organisation, the relationships the organisation has with its customers, suppliers, regulatory bodies and the organisation's overall performance; hence, it is very closely associated with autonomy.

Complexity

Again, complexity itself is not a competence, but refers to the ability of individuals within an organisation to understand the complexities of its products, services and the general business environment, both in the internal and external contexts. Complexity may suggest a degree of uncertainty or unpredictability in how an organisation interacts with others; therefore, making sense of this, and formulating a methodical and often creative approach to problem solving, is key to individuals' abilities in this area.

Complexity also includes the need to understand fully the implications of financial and technical issues and to appreciate the need for balance between time, cost and quality.

Business skills

This is the core competency that carries the greatest emphasis on management skills. Individuals must be able to demonstrate a wide range of attributes, especially in terms of leadership and business acumen. Business skills frequently require a systematic and collaborative approach, and individuals must maintain their awareness of technical and commercial matters; of regulatory and legislative compliance; and to be able to communicate these at all levels both within and outside the organisation at a level of detail appropriate to the audience.

Individuals must also exhibit their ability to manage their own continuous personal development, and, where necessary, that of others; both in terms of direct line management and by mentoring of staff in other departments or areas of the organisation.

These core competencies are assessed at seven levels of skill:

1. *Follow*

    Individuals at level 1 will be able to demonstrate that they have the ability to complete tasks under close supervision. Being at the start of the learning curve, they should not be expected to use much initiative.

2. *Assist*

    Individuals at level 2 will still be on the learning curve, but will be expected to use some discretion and have a wider circle of interaction than those at level 1, particularly in specialist subject areas. They will be expected to work on a range of tasks, and to proactively manage their own personal development.

3. *Apply*

    At level 3, individuals will be fairly skilled professionals and experienced team members. They should be able to complete work packages with milestone reviews only and to escalate problems under their own discretion. They may perform a broad range of tasks, and additionally have some supervisory responsibility, taking initiative and scheduling their own work as well as the work of others.

4. *Enable*

At level 4, individuals will be working under general direction within a given framework and will demonstrate a degree of influence. Being subject specialists, and possibly also team leaders, they may well work on a broad range of complex activities and possess a good level of operational business skills.

5. *Ensure and advise*

At level 5, individuals will be subject specialists and possibly also first-line managers. They will have broad responsibility for direction, supervision and objective setting and will have considerable influence on the organisation. They will undertake challenging and unpredictable work and be self sufficient in business skills.

6. *Initiate and influence*

Individuals operating at level 6 will be practice leaders and possibly also senior managers. They will have the authority for an area of work, setting objectives and influencing policy for a significant part of the organisation. Their work will necessarily be highly complex and strategic, and they will demonstrate an ability to initiate and lead technical and business change.

7. *Set strategy, inspire and mobilise*

Individuals operating at level 7 will also be practice leaders and senior managers. Their authority will include setting policy, making decisions critical to the organisation and influencing key suppliers and customers at senior level. They will take a leading role in determining and directing organisational strategy and will demonstrate a full range of management and leadership skills.

The levels used in the CESG Certified Professional scheme are mostly level 2 for Practitioner roles, level 4 for Senior Practitioner roles and level 6 for Lead Practitioner roles. However, in some cases level 3 is used where appropriate.

Full details of the Skills Framework for the Information Age can be found at http://www.sfia-online.org.

THE IISP INFORMATION SECURITY SKILLS FRAMEWORK

The Institute of Information Security Professionals[3] originally developed its information security skills framework as a means of assessing prospective members prior to interview. The skills are rated at four levels:

1. Skill level 1: Awareness, in which individuals are able to demonstrate a reasonable understanding of the skill area and how it is applied in practice.
2. Skill level 2: Basic application, in which individuals are able to demonstrate not only an understanding of the skill area but also are able to show that

[3] The IISP Skills Framework is Copyright © The Institute of Information Security Professionals.

they are able to apply it to basic tasks, possibly under supervision of a more experienced practitioner.

3. Skill level 3: Skilful application, in which individuals are able to demonstrate not only an understanding of the skill area but are also able to apply it to complex tasks without supervision by a more experienced practitioner.

4. Skill level 4: Expert, in which individuals are generally recognised as authorities who are in the forefront of development of the skill area and are acknowledged experts by their peers in the skill area.

The full IISP Skills Framework document (Version 6.1 at the time of writing) can be downloaded from the IISP's website at www.iisp.org

The skills themselves are in ten distinct groups, each of which is sub-divided as follows.

- Skills Group A: Information Security Management, including:
  - information governance;
  - policy and standards;
  - information security strategy;
  - innovation and business improvement;
  - information security awareness and training;
  - legal and regulatory environment;
  - third party management.
- Skills Group B: Information Risk Management, including:
  - risk assessment;
  - risk management.
- Skills Group C: Implementing Secure Systems, including:
  - security architecture;
  - secure development.
- Skills Group D: Information Assurance Methodologies and Testing, including:
  - information assurance methodologies;
  - security testing.
- Skills Group E: Operational Security Management, including:
  - secure operations management;
  - secure operations and service delivery;
  - vulnerability assessment.
- Skills Group F: Incident Management, including:
  - incident management;
  - investigation;
  - forensics.

- Skills Group G: Audit, Assurance and Review, including:
  - audit and review.
- Skills Group H: Business Continuity Management, including:
  - business continuity planning;
  - business continuity management.

The CESG scheme only makes use of the above eight skills groups – Skills group I (Information Systems Research) is not required by any CESG role, and all the CESG Professional (i.e. non-technical) skills are examined under the SFIA framework rather than making use of IISP skills group J. However, brief details of these have been included for completeness:

- Skills Group I: Information Systems Research, including:
  - research;
  - academic research;
  - applied research.
- Skills Group J: Professional skills, including:
  - teamwork and leadership;
  - delivering;
  - managing customer relationships;
  - corporate behaviour;
  - change and innovation;
  - analysis and decision making;
  - communications and knowledge sharing.

Each of the eight skill groups assessed by the CESG scheme (A to H) are assessed in just the first three of the four skills levels – there is currently no requirement for applicants to demonstrate expert level in any of the roles, although the ability to do so should not detract from an application.

For each role, different skill groups will be required at different levels, and some of these will be absolutely key to the role and are referred to as 'core' competences. Details can be found in the CESG document Certification for IA Professionals which fully describes how the IISP skills framework is used, and can be downloaded from: www.cesg.gov.uk/publications/Documents/cesg_certification_for_ia_professionals.pdf.

Since all applicants are assessed against the skills framework, they should always be able to demonstrate compliance with the skill levels required by providing verifiable evidence of their capabilities.

11 HMG SECURITY-RELATED DOCUMENTS

In this chapter, we will examine the key UK Government documents that relate to information security. The following documents are all key to the overall scheme. Some are free to download, whilst others marked * must be requested from CESG. Links to the online documents are provided in Appendix H.

The HMG Security Policy Framework includes government security classifications. Several of the documents refer specifically to two roles in particular:

- the Senior Information Risk Owner (SIRO) – usually a senior management or board member who understands how the strategic business goals of the organisation may be impacted by information risks; how those risks may be managed; takes overall ownership of the organisation's information risk policy and acts as champion for information risk on the Board;

- the Accreditor – who provides impartial assessment of risks to which an information system may be exposed, and accredits such systems on behalf of the organisation's senior management.

HMG SECURITY POLICY FRAMEWORK

The most recent HMG Security Policy Framework at the time of writing is version 11.0, dated October 2013. It is an unclassified, publicly available document, describes the security controls that must be applied to all UK Government assets and underpins five key government initiatives:

- **the national security strategy**, which identifies four national security policies – counter-terrorism, cyber security, international military crises and natural disasters – and is described in detail in *A Strong Britain in an Age of Uncertainty;*

- **the strategic defence and security review**, which sets out how to achieve the objectives described in the National Security Strategy, and is described in detail in *Security Britain in an Age of Uncertainty;*

- **contest**, the government's counter-terrorism strategy, which consists of four strands – Prevent; Pursue; Protect; Prepare – and is described in detail in *The United Kingdom's Strategy for Countering Terrorism;*

- **the UK cyber security strategy**, which aims to close the gap between the need for digital services and the risks associated with cyber security, and is described in detail in *The UK Cyber Security Strategy, Protecting and Promoting the UK in a Digital World;*

- **the civil contingencies act (2004)**, which covers all forms of civil protection in the UK.

The framework consists of four main security policies, each of which is underpinned by a number of mandatory requirements (MRs). The four policies and their respective MRs are summarised below.

Security Policy No. 1: Governance and Security Approaches

Roles accounting and responsibilities

Mandatory requirement 1
Departments and Agencies must establish an appropriate, suitably staffed and trained security organisation with clear lines of responsibility and accountability at all levels of the organisation. This must include a Board-level lead with authority to influence investment decisions and agree the organisation's overall approach to security.

Mandatory requirement 2
Departments and Agencies must:

- adopt a holistic risk management approach covering all areas of protective security across their organisation;
- develop their own security policies, tailoring the standards and guidelines set out in this framework to the particular business needs, threat profile and risk appetite of their organisation and its delivery partners.

Culture, education and awareness

Mandatory requirement 3
Departments and Agencies must ensure that all staff are aware of Departmental security policies and understand their personal responsibilities for safeguarding assets and the potential consequences of breaching security rules.

Managing and recovering from incidents

Mandatory requirement 4
Departments and Agencies must have robust and well-tested policies, procedures and management arrangements in place to respond to, investigate and recover from security incidents or other disruptions to core business.

These include:

- physical security incidents resulting from either criminality (e.g. forced break-in, terrorist attack etc.) or other hazards (e.g. flooding);
- information breaches – compromise or loss of information through carelessness, theft, insider fraud, deliberate leaking or malicious attack (i.e. espionage);

- cyber/ICT security incidents resulting from electronic attacks, compromise of communications security or disruption of online services.

Assurance and reporting

Mandatory requirement 5
Departments and Agencies must have an effective system of assurance in place to satisfy their Accounting Officer/Head of Department and Management Board that the organisation's security arrangements are fit for purpose, that information risks are appropriately managed and that any significant control weaknesses are explicitly acknowledged and regularly reviewed.

Security Policy No. 2: Security of Information

Information security policy

Mandatory requirement 6
Departments and Agencies must have an information security policy setting out how they and any delivery partners and suppliers will protect any information assets they hold, store or process (including electronic and paper formats and online services) to prevent unauthorised access, disclosure or loss. The policies and procedures must be regularly reviewed to ensure currency.

Valuing and classifying assets

Mandatory requirement 7
Departments and Agencies must ensure that information assets are valued, handled, shared and protected in line with the standards and procedures set out in the Government Security Classifications Policy (including any special handling arrangements) and the associated technical guidance supporting this framework.

Risk assessment and accreditation of ICT systems

Mandatory requirement 8
All ICT systems that handle, store and process HMG classified information or business-critical data, or that are interconnected to cross-government networks or services (e.g. the Public Services Network (PSN)), must undergo a formal risk assessment to identify and understand relevant technical risks; and must undergo a proportionate accreditation process to ensure that the risks to the confidentiality, integrity and availability of the data, system and/or service are properly managed.

Risk treatment – technical, procedural and physical security controls

Mandatory requirement 9
Departments and Agencies must put in place an appropriate range of technical controls for all ICT systems, proportionate to the value, importance and sensitivity of the information held and the requirements of any interconnected systems.

In addition to complying with any pre-defined codes of connection, organisations must apply technical controls that include:

- patching against known vulnerabilities;
- firewall boundary protection;
- policies for content checking and blocking;
- protective monitoring;
- policies to lock down systems to restrict unnecessary services;
- management of user accounts so as to ensure user accountability and the application of minimum necessary privilege.

Mandatory requirement 10
Departments and Agencies must implement appropriate procedural controls for all ICT (or paper-based) systems or services to prevent unauthorised access and modification, or misuse by authorised users.

Mandatory requirement 11
Departments and Agencies must ensure that the security arrangements among their wider family of delivery partners and third party suppliers are appropriate to the information concerned and the level of risk to the parent organisation. This must include appropriate governance and management arrangements to manage risk, monitor compliance and respond effectively to any incidents.

Any site where third party suppliers manage assets at SECRET or above must be accredited to List X standards.

Managing and reporting security incidents

Mandatory requirement 12
Departments and Agencies must have clear policies and processes for reporting, managing and resolving Information Security Breaches and ICT security incidents.

Security Policy No. 3: Personnel Security

Recruitment checks and national security vetting

Mandatory requirement 13
Departments must ensure that personnel security risks are effectively managed by applying rigorous recruitment controls, and a proportionate and robust personnel security regime that determines what other checks (e.g. national security vetting) and ongoing personnel security controls should be applied.

There are three levels of National Security Vetting (NSV): the Counter-Terrorist Check (CTC), Security Check (SC) and Developed Vetting (DV). These must only be applied where a risk assessment indicates that it is appropriate and proportionate to do so, in keeping with the HMG Statement of Vetting Policy. This statement and full details of the baseline personnel security standard (BPSS) and NSV are available publicly on GOV.UK.

Ongoing personnel security management

Mandatory requirement 14

Departments and Agencies must have in place an appropriate level of ongoing personnel security management, including formal reviews of NSV clearances, and arrangements for vetted staff to report changes in circumstances that might be relevant to their suitability to hold a security clearance.

Mandatory requirement 15

Departments must make provision for an internal appeals process for existing employees wishing to challenge NSV decisions and inform Cabinet Office Government Security Secretariat should an individual initiate a legal challenge against a NSV decision.

Security Policy No. 4: Physical Security and Counter Terrorism

Security risk assessment

Mandatory requirement 16

Departments and Agencies must undertake regular security risk assessments for all sites in their estate and put in place appropriate physical security controls to prevent, detect and respond to security incidents.

Internal controls

Mandatory requirement 17

Departments and Agencies must implement appropriate internal security controls to ensure that critical, sensitive or classified assets are protected against both surreptitious and forced attack, and are only available to those with a genuine 'need to know'. Physical security measures must be proportionate to level of threat, integrated with other protective security controls, and applied on the basis of the 'defence in depth' principle.

Building and perimeter security

Mandatory requirement 18

Departments and Agencies must put in place appropriate physical security controls to prevent unauthorised access to their estate, reduce the vulnerability of establishments to terrorism or other physical attacks and facilitate a quick and effective response to security incidents. Selected controls must be proportionate to the level of threat, appropriate to the needs of the business and based on the 'defence in depth' principle.

Preparing for critical incidents

Mandatory requirement 19

Departments and Agencies must ensure that all establishments in their estate put in place effective and well-tested arrangements to respond to physical security incidents, including appropriate contingency plans and the ability to immediately implement additional security controls following a rise in the Government Response Level.

Responding to critical incidents

Mandatory requirement 20
Departments and Agencies must be resilient in the face of physical security incidents, including terrorist attacks, applying identified security measures and implementing incident management contingency arrangements and plans with immediate effect following a change to the Government Response Level.

UK GOVERNMENT SECURITY CLASSIFICATIONS

The government recently simplified its security classification scheme, reducing the number of classification levels from five to three. The old Government Protective Marking Scheme, which had been used for several decades, consisted of: **UNCLASSIFIED**, **RESTRICTED**, **CONFIDENTIAL**, **SECRET** and **TOP SECRET**, and had originally been developed for paper-based information rather than for a mixture of paper and electronic information.

The top two tiers – **SECRET** and **TOP SECRET** – remain, but the lower three – UNCLASSIFIED, RESTRICTED and CONFIDENTIAL – have changed. Unclassified has essentially been removed completely, and RESTRICTED and CONFIDENTIAL have been combined to become **OFFICIAL**.

The government's publication, *Government Security Classifications April 2014*, sets out four principles:

1. that all information collected, stored, processed, generated or shared in order to deliver government services requires an appropriate level of protection;
2. that all government employees and contractors have a duty to safeguard all government information to which they have access, irrespective of whether or not it carries protective marking, and that they must be appropriately trained to do so;
3. that access to all sensitive information should only be granted on the basis of a need to know;
4. that all information assets exchanged with external partners must be adequately protected.

The document defines the three remaining classification levels as follows:

OFFICIAL

The majority of information that is created or processed by the public sector. This includes routine business operations and services, some of which could have damaging consequences if lost, stolen or published in the media, but are not subject to a heightened threat profile.

OFFICIAL information includes that generated by government as a part of its day-to-day business; commercial information, often provided to government in confidence; personal information that must be protected under the DPA.

SECRET

Very sensitive information that justifies heightened protective measures to
defend against determined and highly capable threat actors. For example, where
compromise could seriously damage military capabilities, international relations
or the investigation of serious organised crime.

SECRET information includes that which could place lives at risk; hinder intelligence
operations, including those against organised crime; hinder international relations;
threaten aspects of the critical national infrastructure.

TOP SECRET

HMG's most sensitive information requiring the highest levels of protection
from the most serious threats. For example, where compromise could cause
widespread loss of life or else threaten the security or economic wellbeing of the
country or friendly nations.

TOP SECRET information includes that which could lead to widespread loss of life;
disrupt the stability or economy of the UK or its allies; seriously damage international
relations; cause extremely serious and long-term damage to intelligence operations,
including those against organised crime.

The document continues by defining the special handling instructions that might be
required such as: descriptors, which further specify the sensitivity of information;
code words, which are used to identify specific assets or events; prefixes and national
caveats, which might be used to restrict visibility of information.

Next, the document lists and briefly describes the legal framework that encompasses
the classification system, and references four specific Acts of Parliament:

- the Official Secrets Act 1989;
- the Data Protection Act 1998;
- the Freedom of Information Act 2000;
- the Public Records Act 1967.

It then goes into considerable detail on threat modelling and security outcomes; working
with HMG assets, including comprehensive guidelines for the handling, storage, transfer
and disposal of information assets; and protecting assets and infrastructure, including
security principles and a summary of technical controls.

APPENDIX A
TAXONOMIES AND DESCRIPTIONS

Taxonomies are simply ways of ordering or classifying information, and can help us to understand concepts through either diagrams or written explanations. For clarity, this Appendix includes both forms for the following areas:

- an overall taxonomy of information risk;
- typical impacts or consequences.

It should be noted that these are simply the author's interpretation, and are not necessarily complete in terms of all possibilities, or to the deepest level of abstraction.

INFORMATION RISK

Information risk is the combination of the impact or consequence of a threat or hazard on an information asset and likelihood or probability of its doing so. Figure A.1 illustrates the key components.

Figure A.1 An overall taxonomy of information risk

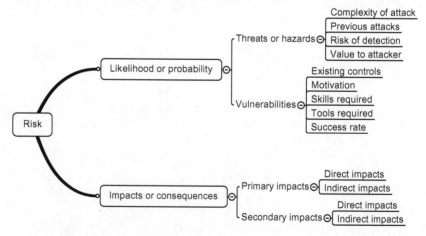

Impact or consequence

The impact or consequence of an event is the successful result of one or more threats acting upon one or more vulnerabilities of an information asset. They are categorised as follows:

Primary impacts. Primary impacts are those that result from the event itself, when a business function is detrimentally affected or unable to continue.

- Direct primary impacts. For example, if a customer database is hacked and personal information is stolen, the organisation will lose control of that valuable information resource.

- Indirect primary impacts. Indirect impacts are those that may occur as a consequence of the direct impact. In the above example, the Information Commissioner may levy a fine against the organisation for failing to adequately protect the information.

Secondary impacts. Secondary impacts are those that result from responding to or recovering from the event.

- Direct secondary impacts include such things as customers purchasing their products or services from another supplier.

- Indirect secondary impacts include such things as fines imposed for failing to file statutory returns on time because the information is unavailable.

See the next section, Typical Impacts or Consequences, for lists and descriptions of various types of impact or consequence.

Likelihood or probability

Likelihood expresses the possibility that an event may occur, but places no certainty on it doing so. Probability, on the other hand, expresses a greater degree of certainty, in that it is based on mathematical or statistical information gathered by research. The two terms are sometimes used interchangeably, but it should be remembered that likelihood is a qualitative view, whereas probability is a quantitative view.

Threats or hazards. Some threats are malevolent in origin, such as hacking and social engineering whilst others are benign, such as environmental threats and simple failures.

The likelihood will be influenced by the following:

- the value of information asset to attacker. In cases where an attack is from a malevolent source, the value of the information asset to the attacker will contribute to the lengths to which the attacker will go in order to carry out the threat;

- the complexity of the attack. Some threats can easily be carried out, especially where automated tools are available to the attacker. Others will require considerably more technical expertise, and are unlikely to be undertaken by so-called 'script kiddies';

- the risk of detection. In the case of some types of attack, the attacker must spend significant amounts of time in carrying out the attack. The risk of detection increases with time, and those attacks that can be carried out more quickly may be adopted more frequently;

- previous attacks. Those threats or hazards that are known to have already occurred will have a considerable bearing on the likelihood of an attack succeeding.

Appendix B lists and describes various types of threats and hazards.

Vulnerabilities are weaknesses in or surrounding the information asset, which a treat may exploit in order to compromise the information asset. Vulnerabilities may be physical, such as inefficient locks; technical, such as poorly configured firewall rules; or procedural, such as a lack of segregation of duties. They have five contributing factors:

- existing controls. The strengths of existing controls will determine the ability of an information asset to resist an attack;

- the motivation of the attacker. This might be either revenge or financial gain for the attacker, or, conversely, it might be financial disadvantage for the information asset owner;

- the technical skills required of attackers to successfully attack an information asset;

- the tools required in order to carry out a successful attack. Many of these are freely available on the Internet;

- success rate. The previous success rate of a type of attack, if this is known.

Appendix C lists and describes various types of vulnerabilities.

TYPICAL IMPACTS OR CONSEQUENCES

Figure A.2 illustrates and describes some of the possible impacts or consequences that might arise as a result of a successful threat against an information asset.

Operational impacts

Operational impacts are felt much more quickly by the organisation. Most are very obvious – for example, when information to which they expect to have access is no longer available, or which they can plainly see has been dramatically altered.

Very often, direct operational impacts will result in subsequent indirect financial impacts, so an inability to meet a service contract may well result in lost orders or claims for contractual damages. Operational impacts include:

- loss of data (confidentiality, integrity and availability);

- loss of premises and equipment;

Figure A.2 Typical impacts or consequences

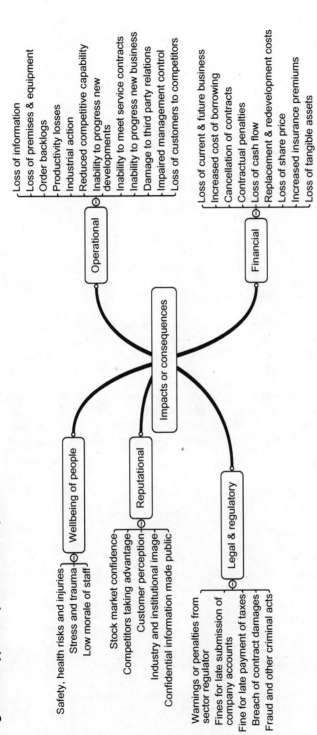

- order backlogs;
- productivity losses;
- industrial action;
- reduced competitive capability;
- inability to meet service contracts;
- inability to progress new business or developments;
- damage to third-party relations;
- impaired management control;
- loss of customers to competitors (churn).

Financial impacts

Unsurprisingly, financial impacts or consequences are normally those that gain the greatest attention within the organisation. It is frequently against a backdrop of possible financial loss that the costs of remedial actions will be compared. Whilst this is certainly correct, it is also true for other types of impact as well.

Many of these impacts – for example, lost sales immediately following the event – will be felt very quickly, whilst others – for example, increased insurance premiums – may not manifest themselves until a later date, possibly some time after the costs of the event have been counted.

Financial impacts may also not be as noticeable to the whole organisation – for example, staff may not be aware of the financial implications of an event at all, and have no appreciation of the position in which the organisation finds itself until they read about it in the media or find that pay increases and bonuses are reduced. Financial impacts include:

- loss of current and future business opportunities;
- increased cost of borrowing;
- cancellation of contracts;
- contractual penalties;
- loss of cash flow;
- replacement and redevelopment costs;
- loss of share price;
- increased insurance premiums;
- loss of tangible assets.

Legal and regulatory impacts

As with reputational impacts, legal and regulatory impacts can have serious repercussions on an organisation, and the handling of these is best dealt with by a specialist team within the organisation, who may communicate information regarding an event through the corporate communication department. Legal and regulatory impacts include:

- warnings or penalties from sector regulator;
- fines for late submission of company accounts;
- fines for late payment of taxes;
- breach of contract damages;
- fraud and other criminal acts.

Reputational impacts

Reputational impacts are almost always highly detrimental to the organisation. For this reason, many organisations employ communication specialists who are skilled in countering negative publicity and putting a positive spin on any bad news. In such organisations, most staff are advised not to talk directly to the media, but to pass enquiries through to the corporate communication department. Reputational impacts include:

- stock market confidence;
- competitors taking advantage;
- customer perception;
- public perception;
- industry and institutional image;
- confidential information made public.

Wellbeing of staff and the public-at-large

Although more rare, safety incidents are generally highly visible outside the organisation, and occasionally have an impact on the public-at-large. More common, however, are any events that may have an adverse effect on the organisation's staff, and these can also cascade into financial and operational secondary impacts. Wellbeing impacts include:

- safety, health risks and injuries;
- stress and trauma;
- low morale of staff.

APPENDIX B
TYPICAL THREATS AND HAZARDS

Threats and hazards cause impacts or consequences to occur on one or more assets by taking advantage of one or more vulnerabilities. Figure B.1 may not be exhaustive, but should provide a starting point.

MALICIOUS INTRUSION (HACKING)

Hacking is a generic term applied to many forms of unpleasant behaviour, although it began as a description of what people did in order to find out how computers worked and how to improve their performance. Hacking almost invariably results in a breach of confidentiality, integrity or availability as hackers use software tools to intercept and decrypt legitimate information, and either steal it or change it.

Since the introduction of the CMA in 1990, hacking is now treated as a crime, since it invariably involves accessing a computer without the owner's permission to do so.

Denial of service (DOS)

Occasionally, hacking is used to deliver DoS attacks, designed to prevent legitimate access to systems, often to make a political point or as revenge for a perceived or real injustice. Associated with hackers are so-called 'hacktivists', such as the loosely connected hacker group 'Anonymous', who sometimes deface website pages or mount DoS attacks. Their attacks follow no set pattern or target, but the end result becomes an availability issue not only for the organisation hosting the targeted website, but also potentially for its users.

Unauthorised access

Most people think of hackers as working from outside the organisation, and although this may be generally correct, there is no reason why someone within the organisation should not be considered a hacker, since their ability to access information from within is much easier than from outside. It is not unknown for criminal gangs to 'plant' well-trained technical staff and security specialists inside target organisations in order to steal information or systems hardware, and such people might be sufficiently well resourced to evade detection during the recruitment process.

With the introduction of the CMA in 1990, hacking (or at least the unauthorised access of someone else's computer) became a criminal offence, since it invariably involves

Figure B.1 Typical threats and hazards

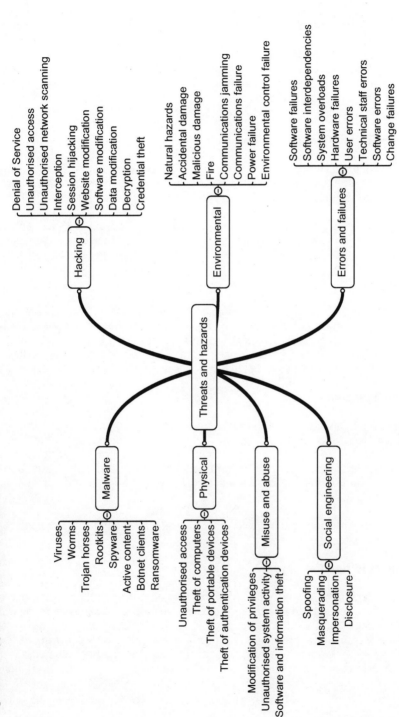

accessing a computer without the owner's permission to do so. Unauthorised use from within an organisation can be considered an offence under the Act.

Unauthorised access to systems and information is not restricted to criminal hackers, and although most prosecutions have been for activities that one would consider unsociable, even people who are supposed to be beyond reproach have been prosecuted for offences under the Act. Some years ago, an ex-police superintendent was convicted of using the Police National Computer System to acquire information about his ex-wife's new partner.

Unauthorised network scanning

Likewise, once hackers penetrate unsecured wireless networks, they will invariably carry out unauthorised scanning of both wired and wireless networks and systems as part of obtaining information that will aid them in attaining their targets.

Once connected to an organisation's internal network, hackers will invariably try to steal user credentials such as user IDs and passwords, and if they can also steal cryptographic keys, they may be able to decrypt information they recover from systems.

Interception

Hackers should not be viewed as unsophisticated individuals. Very often, they are equipped with highly sophisticated tools, allowing them to intercept wireless and wired network traffic, especially in organisations that promote the use of Wi-Fi within their premises. Apart from intercepting Wi-Fi traffic, hackers may also attempt to introduce their own wireless access points in an attempt to lure unsuspecting users onto insecure networks.

Session hijacking

When a user establishes an Internet connection to another computer, the remote computer invariably places a cookie on the user's computer, which permits continuity of the session without the need for the user to re-authenticate at every new request or transaction. This is sometimes known as a 'magic cookie', and if an attacker can obtain this, he can then hijack the user's session and masquerade as the legitimate user.

Session hijacking is quite a complex process and requires an attacker with considerable skill and motivation.

Website modification

Website modification is normally an attack carried out as revenge for a perceived injustice or to demonstrate an attacker's technical expertise. Weaknesses in the website code allow skilled attackers to take control, either of the website page or even the entire website, and substitute information of their own choosing. Individuals and groups of hackers have carried out this type of attack on numerous occasions, sometimes to the great embarrassment of governments and business alike.

Software modification

Attackers who wish to carry out attacks on a large number of prospective targets will often modify existing software by adding their own malicious code – malware – and offer the software through spam emails or other means. The malware might cause a number of different results – for example, to turn the target user's computer into a botnet client or to steal personal information.

Data modification

Attackers who access websites and visibly change the web pages are just one side of the coin. Instead of changing something obvious, such as the website owner's identity, they might modify other data on the website, which might not be so obvious and might provide a visitor with incorrect or misleading information.

Decryption

The unauthorised decryption of encrypted information is a threat that is used in combination with, for example, the theft of business information and the theft of cryptographic keys or the brute-force attack on encrypted information. An example of this is in cases where an attacker will intercept and record encrypted wireless network traffic over a period of time, and either decrypt it having acquired or guessed the correct key, or will subject it to a lengthy attack in order to recover the key, after which further traffic could be decrypted 'on the fly'.

Credential theft

The theft of user credentials permits an attacker to carry out spoofing, masquerading or impersonation attacks against targets. User credentials may be as simple as user ID and password combinations gathered from social engineering or phishing activities. In many cases, attackers will not use the credentials themselves, but will sell them on in bulk to criminal gangs.

ENVIRONMENTAL THREATS

Environmental threats are almost always concerned with availability, since they affect the environment in which a system or information resides. Those impacts or consequences that occur as a result of natural events – for example, severe weather – are often referred to as hazards in order to distinguish their motivation from those of malicious threats.

Natural hazards

Severe weather can knock out power and communications networks, denying us electronic access to our information, and can also have an adverse impact on communications networks that remain operational since many people stay at home during adverse weather, which increases the load on the Internet and delays access to information.

Accidental and malicious physical damage

Whilst physical damage might not at first appear to be a threat to information, instances of accidental damage to underground communications cables is quite commonplace, and in recent years thieves have targeted copper cables for their scrap value. Either instance may well result in an enforced denial of access unless the communications service providers are able to install a fully redundant infrastructure.

It is also commonplace for thieves to mistakenly target fibre optic cables instead of copper cables, the impact of which can be even more severe, since fibre optic cables tend to carry significantly greater quantities of traffic.

Fire

Fire is another serious hazard. Although much information can be backed up in alternative locations, some cannot. Take, for example, the fire in May 2014 at the Glasgow School of Art, in which many students' entire final year work was destroyed. Either the smoke or the water used in extinguishing the fire may have ruined work that was not actually destroyed by the flames. Art is a form of information that is often overlooked, in many cases is very fragile and irreplaceable.

Communications jamming or deliberate interference

Communications jamming or deliberate interference is a less common form of threat to information, but can be highly successful if deployed in a very specific location, and it is an unfortunate fact of life that much of this cannot legally be prevented, since wireless networks operate in unlicensed bands of the radio spectrum.

Many of these hazards affect a wide geographic area, and can cause serious disruption to multiple organisations rather than to a specific organisation or system.

Communications failures

Failures in communications networks can have considerable adverse consequences in the area of availability. Their causes are varied, ranging from accidental damage by utility companies digging up underground cables, cable theft, especially for the copper content in many cables, utility failures in and between communications centres and severe weather, which can quickly disrupt both wired and wireless traffic.

Power failures

Fortunately, in the UK generally, wide-area power failures are relatively uncommon, since the National Grid is extremely robust. However, localised power failures are more frequent due to the nature of network design, since the level of resilience decreases at the lower levels of the network.

In some countries, however, power failures over wide areas are commonplace, and regularly restrict the availability of access to information sources.

ERRORS AND FAILURES

Errors and failures fall neatly into two categories – those made by users and technical staff, and those things that simply fail. Neither form is regarded as being malevolent, even though some user and technical errors are caused by lack of attention or poor training. Despite the view of many technicians that both hardware and software is designed to cause them grief, there is no evidence to suggest that this is actually the case. Examples of error threats include:

Software failures

Software failures are relatively uncommon, since most software is tested exhaustively before it is distributed, and manufacturers usually fix bugs very quickly, since customer satisfaction is normally high on their list of priorities. Software failures are more common when two applications, normally from different manufacturers and which usually work well together, cease to function in the expected manner, usually when one or the other has been updated.

Software interdependencies

As organisations' information infrastructures become increasingly complex, the interdependencies between software applications grow exponentially, and it sometimes only takes a minor change in one to cause a serious downstream problem in several others, hence the need for full regression testing becomes of prime importance.

In 2012, a UK mobile telecoms provider began the rollout of a new customer database, and, despite their best efforts to verify the software before rollout, the software failed under load and almost half their 22 million customers were without service for several hours. There have also been several examples in recent years of High Street banks updating their software, only to find that failures have locked customers out of their online accounts and prevented scheduled transactions from taking place.

System overloads

System overloads are far more frequent, and it is often the case that websites are unable to cope with sudden increases in demand for sales or services. In May 2014, the Ticketmaster website selling tickets for the 2014 Commonwealth Games in Glasgow put an additional 100,000 tickets on sale, and suffered a major overload problem, resulting in people unable to access the site and people who thought they had obtained tickets but had not.

Hardware failures

Hardware failures are much more common than either of the previous examples. Although systems hardware has become increasingly reliable in recent years, failures do still occur, and unless the organisation has invested in resilient systems, duplication of key elements or DR, customers can find themselves unable to access the services they require, resulting in delays, frustration and ultimately bad press for the organisation concerned.

User errors

Errors made by users form a significant threat to information, since it is very easy – using commonly available office applications – to change files or filenames either deliberately or accidentally, to delete files or to change file contents, all with no means of control, and users frequently do not realise their mistakes until long after the event.

Although backup and restoral processes should address this, sometimes the backup media has been damaged or overwritten, and also the user may be reluctant to admit their mistake and request restoral of a file.

This type of failure especially affects shared storage resources including both internal shared drives and Cloud services, where any one of the users sharing the storage facility can inadvertently or deliberately delete or modify files.

Technical staff errors

In theory, technical staff errors should be less frequent than user errors, since technical staff should have received appropriate training for their role. However, mistakes can and do occur, and it is an unfortunate fact that technical staff may well have greater system access privileges, and can do more damage with a single keystroke or mouse click than an ordinary user can.

Internal and external software errors

Generally, all software applications that are used by both large and small organisations have been thoroughly tested for functionality prior to their release, so failures are relatively uncommon but still can and do happen. More prevalent (and potentially more dangerous) in computational software, errors can at best lead to poor decision-making, and at worst could have life threatening consequences, if for example, an application recommended the dosage of a drug to be significantly greater than would be safe.

Change failures

Change failures are often identical to technical staff errors, in that changes are incorrectly made to systems, applications and information. However, the other option here is that changes might have been incorrectly specified, with the possible result that the change either simply did not work as expected, or that the change made matters worse.

This particular type of threat reinforces the need for thorough testing following a change, and also – later in the information risk management process – to examine the results of risks that have been treated to verify that the treatment has been effective and that it has not introduced additional problems.

SOCIAL ENGINEERING

Social engineering is a technique used by hackers and other ne'er-do-wells to acquire information, generally about access to systems, so that their hacking activities are simplified. Social engineering comes in several forms – not only the traditional approach where a hacker attempts to engage with a user by conversation (usually over the telephone or by email), but also by disguising malware as legitimate software and web links and by copying the style, naming conventions and language of a target organisation. For example, they may send a user an email that appears to originate from their bank, but in which embedded web links take the user to the hacker's own website. Examples of social engineering threats include the following.

Spoofing, masquerading and impersonation

Spoofing, masquerading or impersonation is a very common approach to social engineering. It is often achieved by electronic means, in which an email that purports to come from an organisation with whom someone may have had dealings is sent to a number of recipients, but in fact may lead them to carry out an action that captures some of their personal information. Alternatively, it may take them to a website containing (usually false) offers of goods or services, or may infect their computer with malware (see Malware section at the end of this Appendix).

Phishing

Phishing can either be used in the context described above, or as 'spear phishing', in which specific individuals are targeted.

Spoofing, masquerading or impersonation may also take a more personal approach, in which a telephone call is made to the victim inviting them to take some action or other, again usually with unfortunate consequences.

Whatever the method used, the main objective is usually to obtain information that can be used to commit crime – to steal money or to order goods and services to be paid for by another person.

Spam

Spam is a technique frequently used to carry out phishing attacks, by enticing the target to click on a malicious web link or to provide information to the attacker. Many Internet service providers (ISPs) use sophisticated systems to detect known spam email and to quarantine it in a 'spam folder', which the user can then examine and decide whether or not the message is genuine.

Attackers who make use of spam do not care if 99% of their messages are trapped and deleted in this way, since the remainder will reach their destination, and a percentage of these will still be successful.

Disclosure

Disclosure of information is generally accidental in nature, and most social engineering is designed to fool the target into disclosing personal or sensitive information without realising that they have done so.

Most social engineering attacks rely on the fact that target individuals have a fundamental belief that they are either talking to or exchanging information with a genuine organisation.

MISUSE AND ABUSE

Whereas hacking is usually deemed to originate from outside an organisation, misuse normally originates from within. The net result may well be the same for either approach, but in the case of misuse, the internal user or technician has the added advantage of already being on the right side of the organisation's firewall and security systems; may have access to the required passwords and have suitable access privileges. For this reason, the threat from internal attackers potentially presents a significantly greater level of likelihood of success than that of an external attacker. Examples of misuse threats are discussed below.

Modification of system access privileges

Whenever hackers succeed in penetrating a network, one of their first actions will be the modification of system access privileges so that they can explore systems, steal or change information. Naturally, this is much more easily accomplished if the attacker is already within the organisation – actually connected to the network. Systems administrators are generally well placed to undertake this kind of activity, and this frequently takes place as a result of poor control of passwords and the reluctance to change default user IDs and passwords on new systems.

Unauthorised systems activity

Misuse itself can cover a variety of activities, and includes unauthorised system activity, in which users probe systems on an organisation's network to find out what information or software is available to them. It can involve the abuse of other privileges, such as the ability to send email using the organisation's domain name, or, more commonly, abuse the availability of the Internet to download pornography, pirated software, music and films. Inappropriate use of the organisation's Internet connectivity can also result in the organisation becoming infected by malware.

Software theft and business information theft

Misuse can also cover the sending of proprietary information to persons outside the organisation, the theft of the organisation's software, the use of the organisation's facilities to run a business and the posting of derogatory or abusive comments on social networking websites.

Finally, a form of misuse that has also hit the headlines is that of confidential information, or laptop computers containing confidential information, being left unattended – in taxis or on trains, for example. In 2008, secret government documents detailing the UK's policies towards fighting global terrorist funding, drugs trafficking and money laundering were discovered on a London-bound train and handed to a national newspaper and there have also been several reports of government security officials having unencrypted laptops stolen from vehicles.

PHYSICAL THREATS

Many physical threats are also undertaken by employees – many will have access to systems and equipment that they can easily remove from the organisation's premises without the fear of discovery, whereas an external attacker would have to pass through the organisation's layers of physical security in order to do so.

Unauthorised access

Whilst unauthorised access to an organisation's premises in itself is not really a threat, it is what an intruder could achieve once within the perimeter that should concern us. The problem is compounded in cases where a legitimate visitor is left unattended in an organisation's premises, and is able to wander at will within a supposedly secure environment.

Theft of computers and portable devices

Desktop computers are quite difficult to steal, but laptops, tablet computers and smartphones are relatively easy to slip into a briefcase and be taken from a building before the alarm can be raised. However, even the theft of larger computers and racks of servers has been known, and criminal gangs have stolen significant numbers of high-end systems and networking equipment to sell on the black market. With any of these systems, laptops, tablets or smartphones, go the information they hold and quite possibly also details of access permissions to other systems or services.

Theft of authentication devices

The theft of authentication devices is less common, but used in conjunction with a user ID and password or PIN, may allow an attacker easy access to systems, often over the Internet, so that no physical presence on the organisation's premises is necessary.

MALWARE

The term 'malware' is used to refer to malicious software that can be used to attack an information system. Examples of malware include software entities that result in the collection of, damage to or removal of information. Such software is almost always concealed from the user, often self-replicating, attaching itself to an executable programme, and can spread to other systems when the user unwittingly activates it.

Some malware makes no attempt to conceal its existence, appearing to the user as legitimate software. Its purpose, however, is usually very similar in that it may collect, damage or remove information when the user activates what they believe is a legitimate programme. Examples of malware are discussed below.

Viruses

Viruses must always be attached to another piece of software or data – often legitimate – and may be activated by the user opening an email attachment or executing a programme to which the virus has been attached. In the early days of computer viruses, most were harmless, but gradually they have developed to become highly sophisticated and malevolent. Some will encrypt a user's hard drive so that it can no longer be accessed and the user will subsequently receive a demand for money to unlock the encryption. Other users will simply have their personal information stolen.

Worms

Worms are very similar to viruses in terms of what they are designed to achieve, but do so in a rather different way. Worms do not require other software or data to spread, seeking out other targets over networks to which they are connected – and they can do so extremely quickly. In 2003, the Slammer worm is reputed to have infected 75,000 computers within 10 minutes.

Back doors

Back doors provide a means for an attacker to access the computer and use it for their own purposes without the need to undergo any authentication checks. Back doors can be used to turn the computer into a 'botnet client' that can be used under remote control by an attacker to send out spam email or to launch a DDoS attack.

Trojan horses

Trojan horses are much more successful than any other method of attacking a target. These are often disguised as legitimate software or hidden inside compromised files, which users are lured into downloading and/or running. They successfully avoid security countermeasures because users having accounts with administrator privileges allow the Trojan to run.

Another highly successful means of infection is by the use of compromised websites. Trojans can download themselves without the user needing to click on any links on the web page, and the simple act of visiting an infected web page can be sufficient. An increasing number of criminal organisations are making full use of sophisticated Trojans to attack target systems in order to capture information.

Rootkits

Rootkits are more complex software applications that hijack the user's operating system and make themselves invisible both to the user and to any security software. They frequently still perform all operations that the user has requested, but they can also make duplicate copies of sensitive information such as user IDs, passwords and account details and then transmit them to another computer. Rootkits are often used to enable financial fraud or identity theft.

Spyware

Spyware is a common example of the use of cookies by websites, some of which are designed to be persistent and to track and report the user's web usage back to a third party without the user 's knowledge. Some spyware can log the user's keystrokes and search for specific information such as bank account login credentials. Yet other versions have been known to install software that dials premium rate telephone numbers on those computers that are still connected to modems in order to generate revenue for the attackers. Spyware can also be installed by software that performs a legitimate service, such as freeware.

Active content

Active content is the mechanism by which Trojan horses can be downloaded to a computer through its Internet browser. Modern web applications use active code to perform complex tasks within the web page to improve the user's experience. There is no doubt that they are extremely good at achieving this, but they are also ideal for installing malware on a target computer. Failure to set the appropriate level of security in the browser will allow the compromised code to be installed and to run itself on the target without the user's knowledge.

An example of this type of attack is where a banner advert runs on a well known, usually reliable and frequently visited website, in which the html code for the banner has been supplied by a third-party advertiser. The attacker adds the Trojan horse software into the banner html code and people view the website, thinking it trustworthy because of the reputation of the organisation, little realising that the advert is infecting their computer. The payload can be any of the forms of malware described earlier in this section.

Botnet clients

Botnet clients are systems that have been infected with a particular form of malware, which allows a botnet controller to make use of the resource for whatever purpose they have in mind. This might be in order to mount a phishing attack to gain information, to send out large quantities of spam with much the same aim in view, or to mount a DoS attack on one or more websites.

Ransomware

Ransomware is simply another variety of Trojan that downloads onto a computer and generally encrypts user files or the entire hard drive. The malware then notifies the user that their machine can be unlocked after paying a fee. At the time of writing this book, US and UK authorities were warning of a virulent new strain of Trojan that attempted to harvest information from users' machines and if unsuccessful would install and run ransomware instead.

APPENDIX C
TYPICAL VULNERABILITIES

Vulnerabilities or weaknesses in or surrounding an asset leave it open to attack from a threat or hazard. This Appendix lists a number of typical vulnerabilities, but it should be understood that there be many more, and that new vulnerabilities, especially in application software, will be discovered on a daily basis. However, this list, based on BS 7799-3: 2006, provides some generic types and is a good starting point for vulnerability analysis. Figure C.1 illustrates these.

ACCESS CONTROL

Access control has two complementary uses: first, to permit access to resources for authorised persons, and, second, to deny access to those resources to unauthorised persons. Failures in access control are very likely to increase the likelihood of successful attacks against information assets.

Failures in access control are one of the most common methods of successful attacks against information assets, and most are caused either by failures to follow processes or by failure to set up those processes in the first place.

The lack of, or poorly written access control policies

A formal access control policy that is inappropriate for the needs of the organisation, the lack of suitable policy or one that is not properly communicated to staff will cause severe repercussions. Access to systems, applications and information should only ever be given on the basis of the user's business need, and should always be approved by their line management.

Failure to change access rights of users changing role or when leaving the organisation

Another vulnerability connected with this area is that of poor access control for users changing roles or leaving the organisation. The access to systems, applications and information is frequently overlooked when an individual changes roles. A method of combating this is that of role-based authentication, in which the user gains access by means of job function and identity, rather than by their identity alone.

When a user leaves an organisation, their access control permissions should be treated like any other organisation asset, and revoked on leaving or termination.

Figure C.1 Typical vulnerabilities

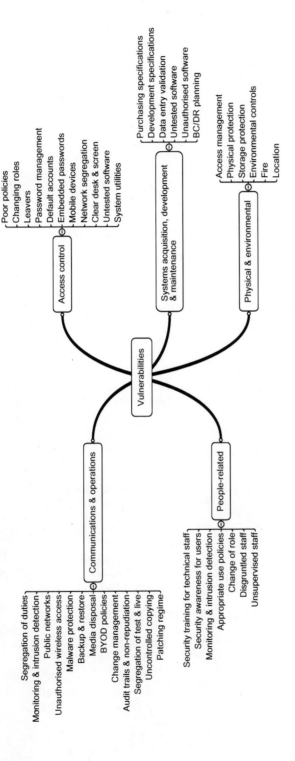

Inadequate user password management

One of the most frequent vulnerabilities is that of poor password management – including the failure to enforce regular password changes – which can be carried out automatically together with a test of password strength, and for those circumstances in which the need for security is greater, additional and robust methods of authentication can be provided.

The continued use of default system accounts and passwords

An extremely common vulnerability is the continued use of default factory-set accounts and passwords for new and upgraded systems. Many individuals in the hacking community are aware of these and circulate them around the community. The failure to change or hide wireless network identities or service set identifiers (SSIDs) will allow an attacker to pinpoint target networks, and if the default administrator passwords have not been changed, or the security level enhanced, these provide a highly attractive entry point into an organisation's network.

The use of embedded system accounts and passwords

Worse still than the continued use of default settings, there may sometimes be a tendency to allow one system to connect to another by embedding user IDs and passwords within applications. This is a highly dubious practice, since a change on one system or another can easily result in application failures.

The lack of security of mobile devices

Many organisations fail to secure mobile devices, whether these are supplied by the organisation or brought in by the users themselves. Mobile devices generally are relatively insecure and easily lost, mislaid or stolen, making both the device and the network to which it can connect equally vulnerable.

The lack of network segregation

Network segregation is commonplace in larger organisations, in which different networks are constructed according to their use, and possibly according to their confidentiality, integrity and availability requirements. For example, an organisation with a significant research capability might well place this on a separate network from finance or general administration use.

Failure to restrict access to networks according to use is a very common vulnerability, and may allow people to reach resources to which they have no entitlement.

Failure to impose a clear desk and clear screen policy

The lack of clear desk and clear screen policy is again a very common vulnerability. Some organisations make it a disciplinary offence for an employee to leave confidential materials in plain view or fail to log out of their workstation when they are away from their desk.

The use of untested software

It.is good practice for organisations to test new or updated software, including the testing of patches, before it goes into a production or general use environment. Untested software may not only cause operational issues if it fails to work as expected, but in cases where it is used in conjunction with other applications, can have a knock-on effect resulting in an embarrassing chain of consequences.

Failure to restrict the use of system utilities

Finally, although a relatively minor vulnerability, the failure to restrict the use of system utilities – normally by setting access privileges within the user's profile – can result in users carrying out activities that are detrimental to their own device or to other systems, applications or information within the organisation.

POOR PROCEDURES

When acquiring systems hardware and software, developing software and maintaining both, it is vital to ensure that selection is carried out according to a formal set of criteria that include appropriate security features. Unlike access control failures, this type of vulnerability is rarely noticed immediately but can result in serious consequences at a later time.

The root cause of this is often a failure to correctly specify appropriate criteria prior to acquisition or development, and may result either from a lack of forethought or a desire to cut costs.

The lack of clear functional procurement specifications

The procedures for acquisition and procurement of systems and services are often very detailed and precise. However, in some cases the specifications can omit vital security requirements that have been overlooked simply because they appear to be an obvious requirement.

The lack of clear functional development specifications

The most obvious example of this type of vulnerability is the lack of, or incomplete, specifications for developers. When specifications are unclear – or even non-existent – some applications developers will make their own judgement call on what is required.

Many years ago, the author was asked to test a system in which the ability to change the system's settings was specified as being subject to 'a complex key sequence'. The developer had no idea what this actually meant, and coded the command exactly as specified. When one typed in the character string 'a complex key sequence', the system opened up access to the settings.

Failure to validate data entry

Many information vulnerabilities are brought about by a failure of applications to test for correctly formatted data, and hackers can exploit this lack of validation to cause failures, which subsequently allow them to inject inappropriate data, take control of applications or steal information.

The use of undocumented software

We have already discussed the lack of or insufficient software testing under access control vulnerabilities, but this is also a systems acquisition, development and maintenance issue, as is that of poorly documented or undocumented software.

The use of unauthorised software

Organisations are also occasionally very lax regarding the uncontrolled downloading and use of unauthorised software, which includes shareware and freeware. If users require additional software in order to carry out their role, this should be available through the correct channels, so that it can be tested and verified as fit for purpose.

Business continuity and disaster recovery planning

The lack of availability of systems and services constitutes a very serious threat to an organisation, and the failure to produce and test robust BC and DR plans is frequently a root cause of this.

BC and DR are closely allied with information risk management, but are complex areas in their own right and therefore beyond the scope of this book. However, a brief description of these has been provided in Chapter 8.

PHYSICAL AND ENVIRONMENTAL SECURITY

Physical security is normally highly visible, both to staff and to potential intruders. Very often, the mere presence of robust physical security is sufficient to deter an intruder, but even so it is important that physical security measures are appropriate and well maintained.

Environmental vulnerabilities tend to be rather more difficult to address but are generally relatively easy to identify and can either relate to the location or construction of premises (for example in a flood plain) or to the environmental subsystems that underpin major premises such as large office buildings, factories, warehouses and data centres.

Poor management of access to premises and to areas within them

Security consultants will often offer to try to gain entry to an organisation's premises as part of a security audit or test. The careless use of physical access control to buildings, rooms and offices frequently makes this a simple task – tailgating behind legitimate staff is one of the most common forms of unauthorised entry.

Inadequate physical protection for premises, doors and windows

Despite the number of break-ins, the lack of, or poor, physical protection for buildings, doors and windows remains a very significant vulnerability that thieves (and approved security consultants) will use to their advantage.

Unprotected storage

Unprotected storage may be a surprising addition to the list, but some organisations simply throw out paper records in the general waste without first shredding them, allowing an attacker to 'dumpster dive' to retrieve information. The media have been very successful in employing this approach to gathering news stories, which are invariably to the detriment of the organisation concerned.

The use of unsuitable environmental systems, including cooling and humidity control

Proper planning for the environmental conditions within data centres of all sizes is not always observed, with the result that computer rooms become seriously overheated, affecting availability. The inadequate control of humidity and extremes of temperature should be a serious concern to organisations, as should the susceptibility of equipment to voltage and frequency fluctuations and the loss of power.

The location of premises in areas prone to flooding

Unfortunately, for many organisations the location of their premises in areas susceptible to flooding has become very apparent in recent months. Locations that have never before been flooded within living memory have felt the impact of the severe weather in late 2013 and the early part of 2014.

The uncontrolled storage of flammable materials

An organisation's vulnerability to damage by fire is another cause for concern. Older buildings built largely of flammable materials, and those that contain stores of highly flammable stock, are chief among these.

The location of premises in proximity to hazardous materials or facilities that process them

Finally in this section, the location of premises in close proximity to hazardous material processing or storage facilities must be considered. One only has to look back to the explosions at the Buncefield Oil Terminal near Hemel Hempstead to realise that, although they were located several hundred metres away from the terminal boundary, several buildings were irreparably damaged by the heat from the fires that ensued.

COMMUNICATIONS AND OPERATIONS MANAGEMENT

Along with access control failures, failures of operations management and communications systems rank high among the vulnerabilities that can be successfully exploited, whether deliberately or accidentally.

Many of these are due to process failures – again; either through failure to observe them or to have them in the first place.

The failure to ensure the appropriate segregation of duties where necessary

The failure to segregate duties where needed can allow attackers to take advantage of access to information which they might not normally have. This ties back into access control, in which access to information might benefit from being role dependent.

Inadequate network monitoring and management including intrusion detection

Inadequate network management, including the monitoring of hacking and intrusion attacks will mean that successful attacks and intrusions are overlooked, and little or nothing is known about their occurrence until it is too late and the damage has been done.

The use of unprotected public networks

Many attacks are caused by unprotected public network connections, which allow an intruder to gain easy access to an organisation's network, including the use of shared computers in public environments such as Internet cafés and the use of unauthorised, and possibly unsecured, wireless access points.

The uncontrolled use of users' own wireless access points

Occasionally, users of an organisation's networks will discover ways of subverting the organisation's security procedures and will attempt to connect their devices to parts of the network to which they have no entitlement. One way in which this is achieved is by connecting in a 'rogue' wireless access point to which they have unrestricted access. One of the main issues with this is that the security settings of such wireless access points might not be as strict as those of the organisation itself, and whilst the users may be able to access the network, so might an attacker.

Poor protection against malware and failure to keep protection up to date

Malware protection software, especially anti-virus software that is not kept up to date, will make an attacker's job much easier. Attackers will take advantage of any means of access available to them, and often are aware of vulnerabilities in applications and operating systems long before a fix is available. Delays in updating these applications leaves an organisation wide open to attack.

The lack of a patching and updating regime

In the same way as the regular updating of malware protection software, the failure to install manufacturers' software patches will leave operating systems and application software open to attack.

Inadequate and untested backup and restoral procedures

Most organisations nowadays carry out regular backups of important information and user data. However, it is far rarer for them to verify that these backups are actually fit for purpose and that information can actually be successfully recovered from the backup media. This again presents a serious vulnerability, since backup media that does not fulfil its objective is just as bad as having no backup regime at all.

Improper disposal of 'end of life' storage media

Once storage media has reached the end of its useful life, it should be properly disposed of. There are numerous stories in the press regarding people who have bought second hand computers only to find that the hard drives still contain sensitive or personal information that had not been securely removed prior to the sale. Some organisations will not allow magnetic media of any kind to be resold, and insist that disposal is irreversible.

The lack of robust 'Bring Your Own Device' policies

The concept that an organisation's staff can BYOD has become very popular, since it can reduce the hardware costs to an organisation. However, the lack of appropriate policies for its use, and the lack of enforcement, can bring about serious breaches of security, especially in situations where other members of a user's family have access to the same device.

In 2010, one organisation was badly affected by a virus that was brought in on a user's own personal computer. The machine had been used over a weekend by the user's teenage son, who had unwittingly accessed a website which contained infected software. The resulting infection took the organisation's entire IT department several days to clear up, and the user (a senior manager) was cautioned. Unfortunately, the same thing happened the following week, and the user was then banned from bringing in his own machine.

Inadequate change management procedures

Inadequate change control can lead to software and patches being rolled out to the user population, new systems, services and network connections being made and redundant systems removed without full consideration (and risk assessment) of the consequences. In smaller networks, change control can easily be vested in one or two people on a part-time basis, but as an organisation's network grows, it may be necessary to employ a full-time team with representatives from multiple business units.

The lack of audit trails, non-repudiation of transactions and email messages

In some sectors, it is vital that online transactions and email correspondence is subject to detailed logging and non-repudiation. In many applications, this audit trail is built in to the operating software, and in the event of a dispute regarding 'who did what', or 'who said what', those organisations that are able to produce clear evidence in their favour will have a greater chance of success than those who do not.

The lack of segregation of test and production systems

Those organisations that employ large-scale systems and application testing prior to rollout are open to problems if they fail to separate test and operational facilities, since users may inadvertently connect to a test system resulting in failed transactions.

The uncontrolled copying of business information

Operational management should also limit the uncontrolled copying of information by users who have no need to access it – again, this is also largely an access control issue, but the identification of such activity may fall into a different management area.

PEOPLE-RELATED SECURITY FAILURES

Whilst some incidents are caused by the failure of systems, software and the supporting infrastructure, the root cause of most incidents is through people who either fail to follow a process or who follow a process that is incorrect. Much of this is accidental, some remains deliberate, but whichever the type, most of it is avoidable to some greater or lesser degree.

The insufficient or inappropriate security training of technical staff

Operational support staff may make errors of judgement or mistakes due to insufficient or inadequate training, not only of the technical functions of their role, but also of the need for security within their day-to-day activities.

The lack of appropriate security awareness training for users

User errors in protecting the organisation's information assets are generally the result of a lack of security awareness, and the organisation may not have considered that even basic security training for users is essential if they are to carry out their role properly and protect the organisation from harm.

The lack of monitoring mechanisms, including intrusion detection systems

We have already covered the need for robust monitoring and intrusion detection systems in organisations, but it is worth restating the need for these, not only to detect unauthorised activity from outside the organisation, but also from within, which carries a significantly greater likelihood of success.

The lack of robust policies for the correct and appropriate use of systems, communications, media, social networking and messaging

The lack of robust policies for the correct and appropriate use of systems, communications, media, social networking and messaging remains a key vulnerability for many organisations, since, without these, there is little or no indication of what constitutes 'reasonable use' by staff, and what they might expect to happen if they fail to behave in an ethical manner.

The failure to review users' access rights whenever they change roles or leave the organisation

Also covered under access control vulnerabilities, and frequently overlooked, is that of the failure to review users' access rights whenever they change roles or leave the organisation, and this may present them with an opportunity to take advantage of situations in which the segregation of duties would normally be implicit.

The lack of a procedure to ensure the return of assets when leaving the organisation

On a similar theme, the failure to ensure the return of assets when leaving the organisation presents a very real opportunity for staff to take away physical assets – for example, laptops, tablets, smartphones and authentication devices – which, combined with the previous vulnerability, might leave the organisation open to future unauthorised access. Further, and equally important, would be their continued ability to access business information to which they have no entitlement.

Unmotivated or disgruntled staff

Unmotivated or disgruntled staff may take advantage of their role within the organisation to steal or otherwise damage valuable information assets as well as physical assets. This kind of vulnerability presents a difficult problem to the organisation since, by the time their feelings become known, the damage may already have been done. Hence, many other factors must be taken into account when finding ways to address this.

Unsupervised work by third-party organisations or by staff who work outside normal business hours

Many organisations outsource or otherwise make use of third-party organisations to carry out specific functions for the business. Inevitably, these organisations and the staff who work for them are provided with access to the outsourcing organisation's network and systems. It is especially important that work carried out by these organisations, or by regular internal staff who work outside normal business hours, does not go unsupervised.

INFORMATION RISK CONTROLS

It is often wrongly assumed that a single control of any kind is sufficient to resolve a risk. In fact, it is frequently the case that more than one control is required, and also of different types. It is conceivable, therefore, that a risk could be reduced by some means, leaving some level of risk that is shared with a third party before the residual risk is accepted. There are three levels of control – strategic, tactical and operational. Figure D.1 illustrates the overall structure of controls.

STRATEGIC CONTROLS

Strategic controls come in four flavours:

- **Avoid or terminate.** Avoiding or terminating the risk can mean either stopping doing the activity, in which case there may well be some residual risk; or not commencing an activity, in which case the organisation may be left with an unsolved problem that the activity was intended to address.

- **Reduce or modify.** Reducing or modifying the risk involves the application of suitable controls that result in a lower level of risk once they have been applied. There may remain some residual risk following treatment.

- **Transfer or share.** Transferring or sharing the risk moves treatment of the risk to a third party who will take action if the risk materialises. Insurance is a common form of risk transfer. However, the organisation that transfers the risk still retains ownership of the risk.

- **Accept or tolerate.** When all other options have been discounted, acceptance of the risk is the final choice. This will also be the case when any of the other three options result in some degree of residual risk.

TACTICAL CONTROLS

There are also four types of tactical control:

- **Detective controls.** Detective controls are intended to identify and notify when a threat is actually having a detrimental effect on an information asset or is about to do so.

Figure D.1 Information risk controls

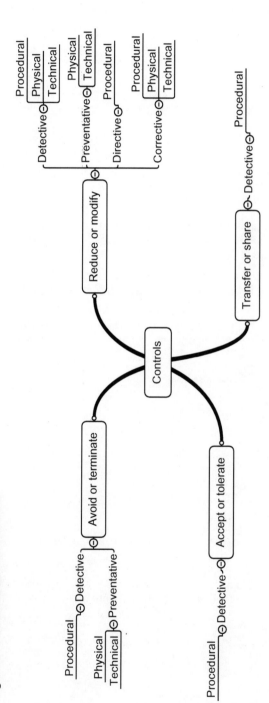

- **Preventative controls.** Preventative controls are intended to stop a threat from having a detrimental effect on an information asset before it has any opportunity to do so.

- **Directive controls.** Directive controls are intended to inform how to stop a threat from having a detrimental effect on an information asset or how to avoid activities that could initiate a detrimental result.

- **Corrective controls.** Corrective controls are intended to prevent a threat from further detrimental activity, to recover from such activity or to prevent it from recurring.

OPERATIONAL CONTROLS

There are just three types of operational control:

- **Procedural or people controls.** Procedural controls dictate how things must be done and include such things as segregation of duties, change control mechanisms and the ongoing monitoring of risk.

- **Physical or environmental controls.** Physical controls protect or change the environment in which information is stored and processed, and include locked doors and CCTV systems.

- **Technical or logical controls.** Technical controls cover the technology-related aspects of information risk management and include anti-virus software and firewalls.

The following sections list the chief controls suggested by:

- The Council on CyberSecurity Critical Security Controls Version 5.0;
- ISO/IEC 27001:2013;
- NIST Special Publication 800-53 Revision 4.

CRITICAL SECURITY CONTROLS VERSION 5.0

A number of organisations, including the UK's CPNI, have published a list of the 20 most critical security controls. This is based upon The Council on CyberSecurity Critical Security Controls Version 5.0.

Whilst this is not a comprehensive list of controls, it does provide a good starting point for organisations that have conducted their risk assessments but are unsure where to begin with risk treatment.

The document may be downloaded from http://www.counciloncybersecurity.org/. The controls are summarised below.

Inventory of authorised and unauthorised devices

Organisations should procure and run software that will scan a network and report on all the devices it finds connected to it. This includes LAN-connected computers, routers, switches, hubs and wireless access points. An inventory is automatically compiled for later analysis.

Inventory of authorised and unauthorised software

Organisations should procure and run software that will scan a network and report on all the operating system and application software it finds on computers connected to it. This can include both Windows PC and Mac computers, and the software will not only automatically compile an inventory for later analysis, but can also track the number of licences held across an organisation.

Secure configurations for hardware and software on mobile devices, laptops, workstations and servers

Organisations should procure and run software that allows them to roll out a standard 'build' to multiple computers, tablets and smartphones by copying across an image of a pre-defined configuration rather than by installing the operating system and individual applications separately, with considerable savings in cost and time.

Continuous vulnerability assessment and remediation

As with the previous three areas, organisations should procure software that will identify operating systems and application software that contain known vulnerabilities and will provide an inventory for later analysis.

Malware defences

Organisations should procure and run anti-virus software. This comes in two forms. First, the 'conventional' anti-virus software that resides on a user's computer, checks for updates and runs a system scan at regular intervals. The second type runs in multi-user systems, such as email servers, and scans incoming and outgoing messages for malware. Both types can be configured either to delete malware or to quarantine it for later examination.

Application software security

Organisations should maintain continuous oversight of software applications, both off-the-shelf and developed in-house, to ensure that it is at the latest (tested) version, and, in the case of commercial software, that it is still under support from the developer. The organisation should ensure that the latest security patches are implemented following successful testing.

Wireless access control

Organisations should procure and run software that allows them to identify all wireless access points operating not only within their premises but also within the vicinity of their

153

premises, since users may inadvertently connect to external wireless access points that appear to belong to the organisation.

Organisations should also examine the inventories collected to identify any 'rogue' wireless access points that may have been introduced onto the organisation's internal network without authorisation.

Data recovery capability

Organisations should ensure that all business-critical information (including configuration information) is backed up and stored in a secure environment, and that information can be restored from backup media when required.

Organisations should also ensure that DR arrangements are in place for those systems that are deemed to be business-critical, and that the switchover facility is tested at regular intervals.

Security skills assessment and appropriate training to fill gaps

Organisations should identify those areas in which detailed security knowledge is required in order to protect the organisation, and ensure that adequate training is provided to staff having those responsibilities.

Organisations should also ensure that all staff are provided with security awareness training on induction and at such times when circumstances dictate that it is necessary.

Secure configurations for network devices such as firewalls, routers and switches

As with the ongoing monitoring of application software, organisations should ensure that the configurations of all network devices, including switches, routers, wireless access points and firewalls, are maintained securely, and that administrative access to them is rigorously protected.

Limitation and control of network ports, protocols and services

Attackers will exploit unsecured ports, protocols and services in order to attack systems, and organisations should run regular port scans, remove unnecessary services and ensure that firewall rules are up to date and render systems less vulnerable.

Controlled use of administrative privileges

The abuse of administrative privileges is a major threat to an organisation's systems, and care should be taken to permit the use of administrative privileges only to individuals who have the specific need to use them, and to remove those privileges when they are no longer required.

Boundary defence

Organisations should ensure that firewalls are configured to reject data originating from or destined for Internet addresses that are known to present a possible threat. Also, organisations should procure and run intrusion detection software that will identify attacks before they can cause harm.

Maintenance, monitoring and analysis of audit logs

Organisations should monitor and record all necessary system and network activities using dedicated software so that analysis of events can be undertaken and that abnormal activity can be identified.

Control access based on the need to know

Having classified their information assets, organisations should restrict access to any of these solely to those individuals or software applications that have a genuine need to access them. Access to sensitive information can be controlled by the correct use of access permissions, or by other means such as separation of information classes by the use of VLANs or by appropriate encryption methods.

Account monitoring and control

Organisations should ensure that user accounts are only created when necessary, and that they are deleted once expiry criteria have been reached. Dormant and locked-out accounts should be reviewed at regular intervals.

Organisations should set and maintain a password update scheme in conjunction with pre-defined password criteria.

Data protection

Having classified their information assets, organisations should ensure that sensitive information is adequately protected by the use of hard drive and/or file encryption, and that any information located in Cloud-based environments is similarly protected.

Further, for personal data, organisations should ensure that the recording, handling, storage and disposal of this information complies with national data protection legislation.

Incident response and management

Organisations should develop and test IM processes to ensure that, when harmful incidents do occur, they have the capability to respond quickly and effectively. The IM process should include containment of, response to and recovery from the incident, and should include appropriate BC arrangements.

Secure network engineering

The design of an organisation's networks should ensure that sensitive information is appropriately protected by the use of DMZ (demilitarised zone) systems and firewalls and network separation, allowing bona fide users access to their resources, whilst denying access to unauthorised entities and attackers.

Penetration tests and 'red team' exercises

Organisations should arrange for regular penetration testing to be carried out to verify that their security arrangements are fit for purpose. Penetration testing is generally conducted on a non-intrusive basis and is designed simply to ensure that security mechanisms are functioning correctly. Additionally, they should consider the use of 'red teams' who take a more intrusive and adversarial approach and take advantage of vulnerabilities to attack systems, although in a non-destructive manner.

ISO/IEC 27001 CONTROLS

Although the primary ISO Standard for information risk management is ISO/IEC 27005, it contains no detailed information on suitable tactical or operational controls for risk treatment, restricting itself instead to the strategic level only. Instead, ISO/IEC 27001 provides an Annex containing a comprehensive list of 114 separate operational level controls, grouped into 14 categories.

A more detailed description of the controls can be found in ISO/IEC 27002 in sections 5 to 18. ISO/IEC 27001, 27002 and 27005 may be purchased from the BSI Online Shop at: http://shop.bsigroup.com

The categories and their associated controls are summarised below.

Information security policies (two controls)

The information security policy controls specify that organisations should define, approve and communicate information security policies to all stakeholders both within and outside the organisation. They also state the need to review these policies at intervals, or if anything changes that might impact on the policies.

- Policies for information security
- Review of the policies for information security

Organisation of information security (seven controls)

This area of controls introduces the need for defined responsibilities within the organisation, along with the segregation of duties in order to prevent misuse and abuse. Interestingly, this area introduces the concept that information security should be considered in all organisational projects, regardless of whether or not they are related to information security.

Additionally, this area deals with the need to address the security of mobile devices and teleworking options.

- Information security roles and responsibilities
- Segregation of duties
- Contact with authorities
- Contact with special interest groups

- Information security in project management
- Teleworking
- Mobile device policy

Human resource security (six controls)

This area deals with three distinct topics. First, those controls required prior to employment, including background checks and the employment terms and conditions that relate to information security. Second, those controls that apply during a period of employment, including the requirement to adhere to the organisation's information security policies, the need for security awareness training and the disciplinary procedures. Third, those controls that apply to the employee's change of responsibilities or when they leave the organisation.

- Screening
- Management responsibilities
- Disciplinary process
- Terms and conditions of employment
- Information security awareness, education and training
- Termination or change of employment responsibilities

Asset management (10 controls)

Asset management controls are concerned with the identification of the organisation's information assets, allocation of ownership of them, their information classification, labelling and handling, their acceptable use and their return when employees leave the organisation.

Additionally, this area specifies controls concerned with the management, transfer and disposal of media, such as memory sticks and DVDs.

- Inventory of assets
- Acceptable use of assets
- Classification of information
- Handling of assets
- Disposal of media
- Ownership of assets
- Return of assets
- Labelling of information
- Management of removable media
- Physical media transfer

Access control (14 controls)

One of the larger topic areas, access controls require a policy that provides for access to network resources to which users have been authorised, the registration and deregistration and access provisioning processes. It goes on to cover the ongoing management of user access rights and their revocation or modification.

Additionally, access control covers the access to systems and application functions, password management and the access to privileged system utility software and source code.

- Access control policy
- Access to networks and network services
- User registration and de-registration
- User access provisioning
- Management of privileged access rights
- Management of secret authentication information of users
- Review of user access rights
- Removal or adjustment of access rights
- Use of secret authentication information
- Information access restriction
- Secure logon procedures
- Password management system
- Use of privileged utility programs
- Access control to program source code

Cryptography (two controls)

Cryptography controls include the provision of a cryptographic policy and the process for cryptographic key management.

- Policy on the use of cryptographic controls
- Key management

Physical and environmental security (15 controls)

Physical and environmental controls begin with those for controlling the physical perimeter of premises together with controls for restricting entry to the premises and areas within it, including secure areas such as computer rooms and less secure areas such as loading bays. It also includes the need to protect the premises from environmental threats and hazards.

The controls continue by considering the siting of equipment, the utilities that support it and the processes for removing it from the premises. Finally, they cover the need for clear desks and screens.

- Physical security perimeter
- Physical entry controls
- Securing offices, rooms and facilities
- Protecting against external and environmental threats
- Working in secure areas
- Delivery and loading areas
- Equipment siting and protection
- Supporting utilities
- Cabling security
- Equipment maintenance
- Removal of assets
- Security of equipment and assets off-premises

- Secure disposal or re-use of equipment
- Clear desk and clear screen policy
- Unattended user equipment

Operations security (14 controls)

Operational security controls focus on formal operating procedures, the need for change and capacity management and the separation of systems used for testing from those in the live environment. They go on to cover malware protection, event logging and the need to synchronise system clocks, the management of vulnerabilities and the requirement to restrict the installation of unauthorised software on systems.

- Documented operating procedures
- Capacity management
- Controls against malware
- Event logging
- Administrator and operator logs
- Installation of software on operational systems
- Restrictions on software installation
- Change management
- Separation of development, testing and operational environments
- Information backup
- Protection of log information
- Clock synchronisation
- Management of technical vulnerabilities
- Information system audit controls

Communications security (seven controls)

Communication security controls deal with the provision of security for networks and network services, and, in particular, they highlight the need to segregate networks carrying different security classifications of traffic.

They continue by describing the need to manage the transfer of information across and between organisations, and include electronic communications, such as email and social networking, and the requirement for non-disclosure agreements (NDAs).

- Network controls
- Segregation in networks
- Agreements on information transfer
- Confidentiality or NDAs
- Security of network services
- Information transfer policies and procedures
- Electronic messaging

System acquisition, development and maintenance (13 controls)

This area deals both with the requirement for information security specifications to be included in the procurement process and how application services and their transactions passing over public networks require protection.

It continues by examining the need for development rules and change control procedures, technical reviews and secure design principles, whether development takes place within the organisation or outside it. Finally, it covers the security and system acceptance testing to be carried out on all systems.

- Information security requirements analysis and specification
- Securing application services on public networks
- Protecting application services transactions
- Security development policy
- System change control procedures
- Technical review of applications after operating platform changes
- Restrictions on changes to software packages
- Secure system engineering principles
- Secure development environment
- Outsourced development
- System security testing
- System acceptance testing
- Protection of test data

Supplier relationships (five controls)

Supplier relationships are key to many organisations' day-to-day operations, and, consequently, the controls in this area relate to security policies and agreements between the organisation and its suppliers. In addition, the controls include the ongoing monitoring of the service delivery and how changes are carried out.

- Information security policy for supplier relationships
- Addressing security within supplier agreements
- Information and communication technology supply chain
- Monitoring and review of supplier services
- Managing changes to supplier services

Information security incident management (seven controls)

Dealing with security incidents requires its own set of controls, which include the allocation of responsibilities for the IM team and the reporting of both incidents and weaknesses within the organisation.

The controls then focus on how incidents are assessed and dealt with, how lessons are learnt that can reduce future risk, and how the evidence (whether physical or electronic) of an incident should be collected, handled and stored.

- Responsibilities and procedures
- Reporting information security events
- Reporting information security weaknesses
- Assessment of and decision on information security events

- Response to information security incidents
- Learning from information security incidents
- Collection of evidence

Information security aspects of business continuity management (four controls)

In this section, we consider the controls required for the planning and implementation of continuity of availability of information services, which include BC, DR and the redundant operation of systems.

- Planning information security continuity
- Implementing information security continuity
- Verify, review and evaluate information security continuity
- Availability of information processing facilities

Compliance (eight controls)

The controls for compliance deal with legal and regulatory requirements and the protection of essential records, how personally identifiable information is handled and, in cases where cryptography is used, how this is managed to ensure compliance with legislation.

Finally, the compliance section deals with independent reviews of the information security position within an organisation, and how individual parts of an organisation comply with its defined security policies.

- Identification of applicable legislation and contractual requirements
- IP rights
- Protection of records
- Privacy and protection of personally identifiable information
- Regulation of cryptographic controls
- Independent review of information security
- Compliance with security policies and standards
- Technical compliance review

NIST SPECIAL PUBLICATION 800-53 REVISION 4

Although the primary NIST publication on information risk management is Special Publication 800-30, it contains no detailed information on risk treatment or the selection of controls.

However, NIST Special Publication 800-53 Revision 4 lists 256 separate operational level controls, grouped into 18 categories in its Appendix F, and also maps them against ISO/IEC 27001 controls in its Appendix H.

The document can be downloaded free of charge from http://csrc.nist.gov/publications/ PubsSPs.html. The categories and their associated controls are summarised below.

AC – access control (25 controls)

- Access control policy and procedures
- Account management
- Access enforcement
- Information flow enforcement
- Separation of duties
- Least privilege
- Unsuccessful logon attempts
- System use notification
- Previous logon (access) notification
- Concurrent session control
- Session lock
- Session termination
- Supervision and review – access control
- Permitted actions without identification or authentication
- Automated marking
- Security attributes
- Remote access
- Wireless access
- Access control for mobile devices
- Use of external information systems
- Information sharing
- Publicly accessible content
- Data mining protection
- Access control decisions
- Reference monitor

AT – awareness and training (five controls)

- Security awareness and training policy and procedures
- Security awareness training
- Role-based security training
- Security training records
- Contacts with security groups and associations

AU – audit and accountability (16 controls)

- Audit and accountability policy and procedures
- Audit events
- Content of audit records
- Audit storage capacity
- Response to audit processing failures
- Audit review, analysis and reporting
- Audit reduction and report generation
- Time stamps
- Protection of audit information
- Non-repudiation
- Audit record retention
- Audit generation

- Monitoring for information disclosure
- Alternate audit capability
- Session audit
- Cross-organisational auditing

CA – security assessment and authorisation (nine controls)

- Security assessment and authorisation policy and procedures
- System interconnections
- Plan of action and milestones
- Continuous monitoring
- Internal system connections
- Security assessments
- Security certification
- Security authorisation
- Penetration testing

CM – configuration management (11 controls)

- Configuration management policy and procedures
- Configuration change control
- Access restrictions for change
- Least functionality
- Configuration management plan
- User-installed software
- Baseline configuration
- Security impact analysis
- Configuration settings
- Information system component inventory
- Software usage restrictions

CP – contingency planning (13 controls)

- Contingency planning policy and procedures
- Contingency training
- Contingency plan update
- Alternate processing site
- Information system backup
- Alternate communications protocols
- Alternative security mechanisms
- Contingency plan
- Contingency plan testing
- Alternate storage site
- Telecommunications services
- Information system recovery and reconstitution
- Safe mode

IA – identification and authentication (11 controls)

- Identification and authentication policy and procedures
- Identification and authentication (organisational users)

- Device identification and authentication
- Identifier management
- Authenticator management
- Authenticator feedback
- Cryptographic module authentication
- Identification and authentication (non-organisational users)
- Service identification and authentication
- Adaptive identification and authentication
- Re-authentication

IR – incident response (10 controls)

- Incident response policy and procedures
- Incident response training
- Incident response testing
- Incident handling
- Incident monitoring
- Incident reporting
- Incident response assistance
- Incident response plan
- Information spillage response
- Integrated information security analysis team

MA – maintenance (six controls)

- System maintenance policy and procedures
- Controlled maintenance
- Maintenance tools
- Non-local maintenance
- Maintenance personnel
- Timely maintenance

MP – media protection (eight controls)

- Media protection policy and procedures
- Media access
- Media marking
- Media storage
- Media transport
- Media sanitisation
- Media use
- Media downgrading

PE – physical and environmental protection (20 controls)

- Physical and environmental policy and procedures
- Physical access authorisations
- Physical access control
- Access control for transmission medium
- Access control for output devices
- Monitoring physical access

- Visitor control
- Power equipment and cabling
- Emergency power
- Fire protection
- Water damage protection
- Alternate work site

- Information leakage

- Visitor access records
- Emergency shutoff
- Emergency lighting
- Temperature and humidity controls
- Delivery and removal
- Location of information system components

- Asset monitoring and tracking

PL – planning (nine controls)

- Security planning policy and procedures
- System security plan update
- Privacy impact assessment
- Security concept of operations
- Central management

- System security plan

- Rules of behaviour
- Security-related activity planning
- Information security architecture

PS – personnel security (eight controls)

- Personnel security policy and procedures
- Personnel screening
- Personnel transfer
- Third-party personnel security

- Position risk detection

- Personnel termination
- Access agreements
- Personnel sanctions

RA – risk assessment (six controls)

- Risk assessment policy and procedures
- Risk assessment
- Vulnerability scanning

- Security categorisation

- Risk assessment update
- Technical surveillance countermeasures survey

SA – system and services acquisition (22 controls)

- Systems and services acquisition policy and procedures
- System development lifecycle
- Information system documentation

- Allocation of resources

- Acquisition process
- Software usage restrictions

- User-installed software
- External information system services
- Developer security testing and evaluation
- Trustworthiness
- Development process, standards and tools
- Developer security architecture and design
- Component authority
- Developer screening

- Security engineering principles
- Developer configuration management
- Supply chain protection
- Criticality analysis
- Developer-provided training
- Tamper resistance and detection
- Customised development of critical components
- Unsupported system components

SC – system and communications protection (44 controls)

- System and communications protection policy and procedures
- Security function isolation
- Denial of service protection
- Boundary protection
- Transmission confidentiality
- Trusted path
- Cryptographic protection
- Collaborative computing devices
- Public Key Infrastructure (PKI) certificates
- Voice over Internet Protocol
- Secure name/address resolution service (recursive or caching resolver)
- Session authenticity
- Thin nodes
- Platform-independent applications
- Heterogeneity
- Covert channel analysis

- Application partitioning
- Information in shared resources
- Resource availability
- Transmission confidentiality and integrity
- Network disconnect
- Cryptographic key establishment and management
- Public access protections
- Transmission of security attributes
- Mobile code
- Secure name/address resolution service (authoritative source)
- Architecture and provisioning for name/address resolution service
- Fail in known state
- Honeypots
- Protection of information at rest
- Concealment and misdirection
- Information systems partitioning

- Transmission preparation integrity
- Honeyclients
- Out-of-band channels
- Process isolation
- Port and I/O device access
- Usage restrictions
- Non-modifiable executable programs
- Distributed processing and storage
- Operations security
- Wireless link protection
- Sensor capability and data
- Detonation chambers

SI – system and information integrity (17 controls)

- System and information integrity policy and procedures
- Malicious code protection
- Security alerts, advisories and directives
- Software, firmware and information integrity
- Information input restrictions
- Error handling
- Predictable failure prevention
- Information output filtering
- Fail-safe procedures
- Flaw redemption
- Information system monitoring
- Security function verification
- Spam protection
- Information input validation
- Information handling and retention
- Non-persistence
- Memory protection

PM – program management (16 controls)

- Information security programme plan
- Information security resources
- Information system inventory
- Enterprise architecture
- Risk management strategy
- Mission/business process definition
- Information security workforce
- Contacts with security groups and associations
- Senior Information Security Officer
- Plan of action and milestones process
- Information security measures of performance
- Critical infrastructure plan
- Security authorisation process
- Insider threat programme
- Testing, training and monitoring
- Threat awareness programme

METHODOLOGIES, GUIDELINES AND TOOLS

The *Collins English Dictionary* defines a methodology as a way of proceeding or doing something, especially a systematic or regular one.

The discipline of risk management has its fair share of methodologies, some of which we describe here.

METHODOLOGIES

CORAS

CORAS is an open-source risk management tool available from SourceForge without the additional scope included in SABSA (see Appendix E, SABSA). It consists of eight discrete steps, which follow the generic risk management principles.

- Step 1 is the initial preparation for a risk analysis. The main objective is to understand what the target is and what the size of the analysis will be.

- Step 2 establishes the overall goals of the analysis and the target to be analysed. The objective is to achieve a common understanding of the target, and the major areas of concern.

- Step 3 aims to ensure a common understanding of the target of analysis, including its focus, scope and main assets. This step will conduct a rough, high-level analysis to identify major threat scenarios, vulnerabilities and enterprise level risks.

- Step 4 aims to ensure that the background documentation for the rest of the analysis, including the target, focus and scope, is correct and complete and is approved. Furthermore, Step 4 includes the risk evaluation criteria decisions for each asset. This analysis step concludes the context establishment.

- Step 5 is the risk identification using structured brainstorming. The risk identification involves a systematic identification of threats, unwanted incidents, threat scenarios and vulnerabilities with respect to the identified assets. The results are documented by means of CORAS threat diagrams.

- Step 6 aims to determine the risk level of the risks that are represented by the identified unwanted incidents.

- Step 7 aims to decide which of the identified risks are acceptable, and which of the risks must be further evaluated for possible treatment.

- Step 8 is concerned with the identification and analysis of treatments. The risks that are found to be unacceptable are evaluated to find means to reduce them. Since treatments can be costly, they are assessed with respect to their cost-benefit, before a final treatment plan is made.

The platform-independent CORAS risk management tool is available as a free download from coras.sourceforge.net, as is a guided tour of the CORAS method.

CRAMM

The CCTA Risk Analysis and Management Method (CRAMM) was developed in 1987 by the UK Government Central Computing and Telecommunications Agency, part of the Office of Government Commerce since 2000.

CRAMM is free to download, but users must obtain a licence from the supplier, Siemens Enterprise Communications.

CRAMM consists of three distinct stages.

- Stage 1. The establishment of the objectives for security by: defining the boundary for the study; identifying and valuing the physical assets that form part of the system; determining the 'value' of the data held, by interviewing users about the potential business impacts that could arise from unavailability, destruction, disclosure or modification; and identifying and valuing the software assets that form part of the system.
- Stage 2. The assessment of the risks to the proposed system and the requirements for security by: identifying and assessing the type and level of threats that may affect the system; assessing the extent of the system's vulnerabilities to the identified threats; and combining threat and vulnerability assessments with asset values to calculate measures of risks.
- Stage 3. Identification and selection of countermeasures that are commensurate with the measures of risks calculated in Stage 2.

CRAMM contains a very large countermeasure library consisting of more than 3,000 detailed countermeasures organised into over 70 logical groupings.

Less complex than SABSA and OCTAVE, it is widely used and is particularly favoured by UK Government departments.

Currently, the links to the Siemens Insight Consulting CRAMM web pages do not work. The Author has endeavoured to discover whether Siemens Insight Consulting still licence and support CRAMM, but has been unable to do so at the time of writing.

FAIR

Factor. Analysis of Information Risk (FAIR), is a framework developed by Risk Management Insight (http://www.riskmanagementinsight.com).

FAIR follows a similar route to risk assessment as other methodologies, but uses slightly different terminology together with its method of deriving the likelihood of an event. It carries out the risk assessment in a different order and consists of four stages.

- Stage 1 – Identify scenario components (much the same as asset identification):
  - Identify the asset at risk.
  - Identify the threat community under consideration. The threat community is used to group different threat sources together, such as internal staff or the hacking community.
- Stage 2 – Evaluate the loss event frequency (the likelihood):
  - Estimate the probable threat event frequency, which it defines as 'The probable frequency, within a given timeframe, that a threat agent will act against an asset'.
  - Estimate the threat capability, 'The probable level of force that a threat agent is capable of applying against an asset'.
  - Estimate the strength of existing controls, 'The expected effectiveness of controls, over a given timeframe, as measured against a baseline level of force'.
  - Derive the vulnerability, 'The probability that an asset will be unable to resist the actions of a threat agent'.
  - Derive the loss event frequency, 'The probable frequency, within a given timeframe, that a threat agent will inflict harm upon an asset'.
- Stage 3 – Evaluate probable loss magnitude (the impact or consequence):
  - Estimate worst-case loss.
  - Estimate probable loss.
- Stage 4 – Derive and articulate risk (the risk analysis):
  - Derive and articulate risk, 'The probable frequency and probable magnitude of future loss'.

Although FAIR covers risk assessment, it does not address an organisation's risk appetite or tolerance and makes no mention of risk treatment, and so is only really useful for the earlier stages of an information risk management programme.

A comprehensive description of FAIR is available from: http://www.riskmanagementinsight.com/media/docs/FAIR_introduction.pdf

IRAM

The Information Risk Analysis Method (IRAM) has been developed by the Information Security Forum (ISF), and is only available to ISF member organisations.

It forms a part of the ISF information risk management approach:

- define;
- implement;

- evaluate;
- enhance.

Using the ISF *Forum Standard of Good Practice*, the Define stage takes account of the organisation's risk appetite and the commitment of senior management to the principle of sound information governance. In the Implement stage, risks at the application, business process or business unit level are assessed, the security requirements are identified and appropriate controls to treat them are selected using the Standard.

IRAM operates in three phases:

1. business impact assessment, which delivers business impact rating forms and a business impact assessment summary;
2. threat and vulnerability assessment, which delivers a threat assessment report, a vulnerability assessment report and a detailed security requirements report;
3. control selection, which delivers a control evaluation report and a control selection report.

In the Evaluate stage, the ISF's annual Benchmark survey is used by members to identify areas of control weaknesses and gaps and to compare their own risk management capability with that of their peer organisations.

Finally, in the Enhance stage, and again using the Benchmark survey and the Standard, members can refine their risk treatment arrangements to increase their level of protection.

More information is available from: https://www.securityforum.org/tools/isf-risk-manager/

OCTAVE

Operationally Critical Threat, Asset and Vulnerability Evaluation (OCTAVE) originates from the Carnegie Mellon Software Engineering Institute.

The OCTAVE method uses a three-phased approach to examine organisational and technology issues, assembling a comprehensive picture of the organisation's information security needs. It is aimed at organisations with more than around 300 people. The method is organised into a progressive series of workshops, and the process is supported with guidance, worksheets and questionnaires.

In the first phase, the organisation builds asset-based profiles, identifying assets, threats, current practices, organisational vulnerabilities and security requirements.

This is achieved in four distinct processes:

1. Identify senior management knowledge.
2. Identify operational area management knowledge.
3. Identify staff knowledge.
4. Create threat profiles.

Moving to the second phase, which involves two processes, the organisation will identify infrastructure vulnerabilities:

5. Identify key components.
6. Evaluate selected components and establish technical vulnerabilities.

In the third and final phase, the organisation will develop security strategies and plans:

7. Conduct risk analysis.
8. Develop protection strategy.

The method then uses a catalogue of practices to apply appropriate controls.

- Strategic practices (SP):
  - Security awareness and training (SP1).
  - Security strategy (SP2).
  - Security management (SP3).
  - Security policies and regulations (SP4).
  - Collaborative security management (SP5).
  - Contingency planning and disaster recovery (SP6).
- Operational practices (OP):
  - Physical security (OP1): physical security plans and procedures; physical access control; monitoring and auditing physical security.
  - Information technology security (OP2): system and network management; system administration tools; monitoring and auditing IT security; authentication and authorisation; vulnerability management; encryption; security architecture and design.
  - Staff security (OP3): incident management; general staff practices.

OCTAVE-S

Whereas OCTAVE relies on a progressive series of workshops involving managers from different levels within the organisation, OCTAVE-S, which is designed for organisations with fewer than 100 people, uses the skills and experience of a smaller team of people (typically three to five in number) who have extensive knowledge of the organisation.

It also differs from OCTAVE in that the OCTAVE-S worksheets and guidance already contain security concepts, which permits less experienced information risk management practitioners to assess a very broad range of risks, many of which may be unfamiliar to them.

Finally, OCTAVE-S is less demanding on information relating to the organisation's information infrastructure, since smaller organisations tend to have less capability to use vulnerability tools.

OCTAVE Allegro

OCTAVE Allegro is a more streamlined version of OCTAVE, and takes a slightly different approach again from OCTAVE in that, although it makes use of progressive workshops, the focus is more on the information assets themselves, the use to which they are put, stored, transported and processed and how they are impacted by threats, vulnerabilities and disruptions.

The method consists of four stages:

- Stage 1: Establish drivers.
  - Establish risk measurement criteria.
- Stage 2: Profile assets.
  - Develop information asset profile.
  - Identify information asset containers.
- Stage 3: Identify threats.
  - Identify areas of concern.
  - Identify threat scenarios.
- Stage 4: Identify and mitigate risks.
  - Identify risks.
  - Analyse risks.
  - Select mitigation approach.

Information on all three OCTAVE methodologies can be found at: http://www.cert.org/resilience/products-services/octave/

SABSA

Developed by John Sherwood in 1995, and published in 1996 as *SABSA: A Method for Developing the Enterprise Security Architecture and Strategy*, the SABSA (Sherwood Applied Business Security Architecture) framework has evolved as a 'best practice' method for delivering cohesive information security solutions to enterprises. It is a six-layer model covering all four parts of the IT lifecycle: strategy, design, implementation and management and operations.

This makes SABSA a very powerful tool that is not limited just to risk management, is designed to ensure that the security needs of enterprises are met, that security services are designed, delivered, and supported as an integral part of an IT management infrastructure and provides guidance for aligning architecture with business value.

SABSA looks at security architecture from a number of different perspectives:

- the business view, referred to as the contextual security architecture, which examines the business assets, risks, processes, organisation, geography and time dependencies;

- the architect's view, referred to as the conceptual security architecture, which examines the strategic and risk management objectives and the organisation's high-level roles and responsibilities;

- the designer's view, referred to as the logical security architecture, which examines the policies and logical security services such as: authentication, confidentiality and integrity protection, non-repudiation and system assurance; people; their roles and responsibilities: and the security domains;

- the builder's view, referred to as the physical security architecture, which examines the business data model, rules, security mechanisms, people dependencies and security technology infrastructure;

- the tradesman's view, referred to as the component security architecture, which examines the standards, tools and products used to implement the overall security architecture;

- cutting across all these is the service manager's view, referred to as the security service management architecture, which examines the delivery management, operational risk management, personnel management and environmental management of the security infrastructure.

Each of these security architectures is mapped against a series of basic questions: what?, why?, how?, who?, where? and when? to form the SABSA Matrix.

SABSA mimics the PDCA model as its lifecycle, but names the parts slightly differently as 'Strategy and planning; Design; Implement; Manage and measure'. It then examines the use of business attributes to provide a link between the organisation's business requirements and the technology and process design, either in the form of ICT business attributes or general business attributes.

- ICT attributes:
  - user attributes;
  - management attributes;
  - operational attributes;
  - risk management attributes;
  - legal and regulatory attributes;
  - technical strategy attributes;
  - business strategy attributes.
- high-level general business attributes:
  - financial;
  - physical;
  - human;
  - process;
  - strategic;
  - system.

In terms of the generic information risk management method, SABSA also includes the processes to provide consultation and communication, referred to as 'communicate', and monitor and review, referred to as 'assure', and has the capability to do this at four distinct levels.

More information on SABSA is available from: http://www.sabsa.org

OTHER GUIDELINES AND TOOLS

BS 7799-3

BS 7799-3:2006 – *Information Security Management Systems. Guidelines for Information Security Risk Management.*

Because of its age, BS 7799-3 is a largely neglected standard, but it does summarise the information risk management process extremely well, with numerous references to the ISO IEC 27001:2005 standard, which was updated in 2012. It is well worth obtaining a copy as background reference material.

Its risk assessment section (5) includes:

- the risk assessment process;
- asset identification;
- identification of legal and business requirements;
- asset valuation;
- identification of implemented controls, threats and vulnerabilities;
- assessment of threats and vulnerabilities;
- risk calculation and evaluation;
- the risk assessor.

In risk treatment and decision-making (6), it describes the processes for:

- decision-making;
- reducing the risk;
- knowingly and objectively accepting the risk;
- transferring the risk;
- avoiding the risk;
- residual risk;
- risk treatment planning.

Finally, it discusses ongoing risk management activities (7):

- ongoing security risk management;
- maintenance and monitoring;
- management reviews;
- risk reviews and re-assessments;
- audits;
- documentation controls;
- corrective and preventative action;
- reporting and communications;
- the role of the security risk manager.

The appendices include:

- A: legal and regulatory compliance;
  - legal framework;
  - national security;
  - corporate governance;
  - electronic commerce, legal framework;
  - identity theft, data protection;
  - IP protection;
  - sector-specific regulations.
- B: information security risks and organisational risks;
  - organisational processes and interrelationships;
  - organisational risk;
  - corporate governance.
- C: very comprehensive lists of examples of;
  - asset identification;
  - example list of threats;
  - threat examples and ISO/IEC 17799:2005;
  - vulnerability examples and ISO/IEC 17799:2005;
  - examples of risk assessment methods.
- D: risk management tools;
- E: relationship between and ISO/IEC 27001:2005 and BS 7799-3:2006.

BS 7799-3:2006 can be obtained in PDF or hard copy formats from the BSI online shop: http://www.bsigroup.com/shop

NIST SP800-30

Guide for Conducting Risk Assessments – NIST Special Publication 800-30 Revision 1.

Whilst there are some minor differences in the approach of SP800-30 from those described elsewhere in this book, it remains an extremely comprehensive and detailed information risk management standard.

One of the most useful sections is its final two-page Appendix L 'Summary of tasks':

- Step1: Prepare for risk assessment.
  - Identify purpose.
  - Identify scope.
  - Identify assumptions and constraints.
  - Identify information sources.
  - Identify risk model and analytic approach.
- Step 2: Conduct risk assessment.
  - Identify threat sources.
  - Identify threat events.
  - Identify vulnerabilities and predisposing conditions.
  - Determine likelihood.
  - Determine impact.
  - Determine risk.
- Step 3: Communicate and share risk assessment results.
  - Communicate risk assessment results.
  - Share risk-related information.
- Step 4: Maintain risk assessment.
  - Monitor risk factors.
  - Update risk assessment.

The remainder of the standard consists of:

- the fundamentals (2);
  - risk management process;
  - risk assessment;
  - key risk concepts;
  - application of risk assessments.
- the process (3);
  - preparing for the risk assessment;
  - conducting the risk assessment;

- communicating and sharing risk assessment information;
- maintaining the risk assessment.

Appendix A	References.
Appendix B	Glossary.
Appendix C	Acronyms.
Appendix D	Threat sources.
Appendix E	Threat events.
Appendix F	Vulnerabilities and predisposing conditions.
Appendix G	Likelihood of occurrence.
Appendix H	Impact.
Appendix I	Risk determination.
Appendix J	Informing risk response.
Appendix K	Risk assessment reports.
Appendix L	Summary of tasks (listed above).

As with all NIST standards, they may be downloaded free of charge from: http://csrc.nist.gov/publications/PubsSPs.html

Risk assessment tools

The Internet lists numerous risk management software tools, many of which are not especially well-suited to use in information risk management, some of which are aimed at the larger enterprise, whilst others can be better used by smaller organisations.

The author does not intend to endorse or make any recommendations as to which (if any) of the tools are best suited to information risk management use, but instead has provided some suggestions as to the key attributes that may be considered. Please note that these do not include the 'usual' considerations, such as cost and support capability, etc.

- Does the tool address any or all of the standards to which the organisation is working?
- Does the tool provide a complete risk management overview, or is it limited to risk assessment only (i.e. no risk treatment)?
- Does the tool contain pre-defined:
  - types of asset?
  - types of impact?
  - threats?
  - vulnerabilities?
  - controls?
- Can additional ones be user-defined?
- Can the tool import an asset list from a spreadsheet or database?

- Does the tool permit the user to break down the impact assessment by confidentiality, integrity and availability?
- Does the tool permit more than one threat or vulnerability for each asset?
- Does the tool permit more than one control for each risk identified?
- Does the tool provide output in the form of a risk register?
- Does the tool provide output in graphical form?
- Is the tool scalable to enterprise level?
- Is the tool single-user or multi-user?
- Can the tool be run on multiple operating systems (e.g. Windows, Mac, Unix and Linux), and are there mobile applications (e.g. iPhone, iPad, Android) that can interwork with it?
- Can a trial version of the tool be downloaded?

APPENDIX F
TEMPLATES

The following templates may be used as a basis for carrying out risk assessments:

- Impact Assessment template.
- Threat Assessment template.
- Vulnerability Assessment template.
- Existing Controls Assessment template.
- Risk Register template.

Figure F.1 Typical impact assessment template

Impact/Asset			Date	
Asset owner			Analyst	
Asset location			Reference	
	Primary impacts		Secondary impacts	
	Direct impacts	Indirect impacts	Direct impacts	Indirect impacts
Operational				
Score				
Legal and regulatory				
Score				
Reputational				
Score				
People-related				
Score				
Financial				
Score				
Total financial impact				
Total impact rating				

VH = Very High   H = High   M = Medium   L = Low   VL = Very Low

Figure F.2 Typical threat assessment template

Date		Reference	
Threat description			
Hacking			
Environmental threats and hazards			
Errors and failures			
Social engineering			
Misuse and abuse			
Physical threats			
Malware			
Operating systems affected			
Applications affected			
Information types affected			
Previous attack history (if known)			
Previous success rate (if known)			
Attack motivation (if known)			

Figure F.3 Typical vulnerability assessment template

Date			Reference	
		Vulnerability description		
Access control				
Systems acquisition, development and maintenance				
Physical and environmental				
People-related				
Communications and operations				
Operating systems affected				
Applications affected				
Information types affected				
Previous attack history (if known)				
Previous success rate (if known)				
Attack motivation (if known)				

Figure F.4 Typical existing controls assessment template

Date			Reference	
Description of controls				
Asset name				
Asset location				
Preventative controls	Physical or environmental			
	Technical or logical			
Detective controls	Physical or environmental			
	Technical or logical			
	Procedural or people			
Directive controls	Procedural or people			
Corrective controls	Physical or environmental			
	Technical or logical			
	Procedural or people			

Figure F.5 Typical risk register template

Information Risk Register

Reference	Date added	Asset name	Asset owner	Brief description of risk	Inherent risk			Treatment *	Recommended control(s)	Control owner	Date due	Residual risk			Next review date
					Impact	Likelihood	Risk level					Impact	Likelihood	Risk level	

Treatment: X = Avoid; S = Share; R = Reduce; A = Accept

APPENDIX G
HMG CYBER SECURITY GUIDELINES

We have stated already that information risk management is not only about cyber security, but that it also encompasses other areas, especially including the risks associated with people who, at the end of the day, are actually the cause of most of the information security problems. That said, cyber security will remain a key part of the information risk management programme for many organisations, and it would be highly remiss to ignore it.

Chapter 11 dealt with the way in which the UK Government deals with information risk management in its own environment. In June 2014 HMG launched a new scheme to improve and promote cyber security, its primary objective being 'to make the UK a safer place to conduct business online'.

First, let us take a very brief look at what cyber security actually is. The UK's Cyber Security Strategy, 2011, defines cyberspace as:

> Cyberspace is an interactive domain made up of digital networks that is used to store, modify and communicate information. It includes the Internet, but also other information systems that support our businesses, infrastructure and services.

We can therefore suggest that cyber security is the art or science of protecting this infrastructure against accidental or deliberate loss or harm.

There are two separate government initiatives:

- The HMG Cyber Essentials Scheme from the Department for Business, Innovation and Skills (BIS).
- 10 Steps to Cyber Security, produced jointly by GCHQ, BIS and CPNI.

Much of the detail of the HMG Cyber Essentials scheme is a copy-and-paste from the documentation.

HMG CYBER ESSENTIALS SCHEME

The Cyber Essentials scheme defines a set of controls which, when properly implemented, will provide organisations with basic protection from the most prevalent forms of threats coming from the Internet. In particular, it focuses on threats which require low levels of attacker skill, and which are widely available online.

Risk management is the fundamental starting point for organisations to take action to protect their information. However, given the nature of the threat, Government believes that action should begin with a core set of security controls, which all organisations – large and small – should implement. Cyber Essentials defines what these controls are.

The scheme provides for two distinct levels of certification:

- Cyber Essentials certification is awarded on the basis of a verified self-assessment. An organisation undertakes their own assessment of their implementation of the Cyber Essentials control themes via a questionnaire, which is approved by a senior executive such as the CEO. This questionnaire is then verified by an independent Certification Body to assess whether an appropriate standard has been achieved, and certification can be awarded. This option offers a basic level of assurance and can be achieved at low cost.

- Cyber Essentials Plus offers a higher level of assurance through the external testing of the organisation's cyber security approach. Given the more resource intensive nature of this process, it is anticipated that Cyber Essentials Plus will cost more than the foundation Cyber Essentials certification.

The scheme recommends the use of controls in five separate areas:

- boundary firewalls and Internet gateways;

- secure configuration;

- user access control;

- malware protection;

- patch management.

Boundary firewalls and Internet gateways

One or more firewalls (or equivalent network device) should be installed on the boundary of the organisation's internal network(s). As a minimum:

- The default administrative password for any firewall (or equivalent network device) should be changed to an alternative, strong password.

- Each rule that allows network traffic to pass through the firewall (e.g. each service on a computer that is accessible through the boundary firewall) should be subject to approval by an authorised individual and documented (including an explanation of business need).

- Unapproved services, or services that are typically vulnerable to attack (such as server message block (SMB), NetBIOS, tftp, RPC, rlogin, rsh or rexec), should be disabled (blocked) at the boundary firewall by default.

- Firewall rules that are no longer required (e.g. because a service is no longer required) should be removed or disabled in a timely manner.

- The administrative interface used to manage boundary firewall configuration should not be accessible from the Internet.

Secure configuration

Computers and network devices (including wireless access points) should be securely configured. As a minimum:

- Unnecessary user accounts (e.g. Guest accounts and unnecessary administrative accounts) should be removed or disabled.
- Any default password for a user account should be changed to an alternative, strong password.
- Unnecessary software (including application, system utilities and network services) should be removed or disabled.
- The auto-run feature should be disabled (to prevent software programs running automatically when removable storage media is connected to a computer or when network folders are accessed).
- A personal firewall (or equivalent) should be enabled on desktop PCs and laptops, and configured to disable (block) unapproved connections by default.

User access control

User accounts should be managed through robust access control. As a minimum:

- All user account creation should be subject to a provisioning and approval process.
- Special access privileges should be restricted to a limited number of authorised individuals.
- Details about special access privileges (e.g. the individual and purpose) should be documented, kept in a secure location and reviewed on a regular basis (e.g. quarterly).
- Administrative accounts should only be used to perform legitimate administrative activities, and should not be granted access to email or the Internet.
- Administrative accounts should be configured to require a password change on a regular basis (e.g. at least every 60 days).
- Each user should authenticate using a unique username and strong password before being granted access to applications, computers and network devices.
- User accounts and special access privileges should be removed or disabled when no longer required (e.g. when an individual changes role or leaves the organisation) or after a pre-defined period of inactivity (e.g. 3 months).

Malware protection

The organisation should implement robust malware protection on exposed computers. As a minimum:

- Malware protection software should be installed on all computers that are connected to or capable of connecting to the Internet.

- Malware protection software (including program code and malware signature files) should be kept up to date (e.g. at least daily, either by configuring it to update automatically or through the use of centrally managed deployment).

- Malware protection software should be configured to scan files automatically upon access (including when downloading and opening files, accessing files on removable storage media or a network folder) and scan web pages when being accessed (via a web browser).

- Malware protection software should be configured to perform regular scans of all files (e.g. daily).

- Malware protection software should prevent connections to malicious websites on the Internet (e.g. by using website blacklisting).

Patch management

Software should be kept up to date. As a minimum:

- Software running on computers and network devices that are connected to or capable of connecting to the Internet should be licensed and supported (by the software vendor or supplier of the software) to ensure security patches for known vulnerabilities are made available.

- Updates to software (including operating system software and firmware) running on computers and network devices that are connected to or capable of connecting to the Internet should be installed in a timely manner (e.g. within 30 days of release or automatically when they become available from vendors).

- Out-of-date software (i.e. software that is no longer supported) should be removed from computer and network devices that are connected to or capable of connecting to the Internet.

- All security patches for software running on computers and network devices that are connected to or capable of connecting to the Internet should be installed in a timely manner (e.g. within 14 days of release or automatically when they become available from vendors).

The Cyber Essentials Requirements document contains three useful links: to the ISF for its *Standard of Good Practice*; to IASME (Information Assurance for Small and Medium Enterprises); and to the '10 Steps to Cyber Security' web pages.

The final section of the document provides a cross-reference between the five areas of controls and ISO/IEC 27001/2, the ISF *Standard of Good Practice*, the IASME standard and the '10 Steps to Cyber Security' recommendations.

There are three documents currently available:

- *Cyber Essentials Scheme: Summary.*

- *Cyber Essentials Scheme: Requirements for basic technical protection from cyber attacks.*

- *Cyber Essentials Scheme: Assurance Framework.*

10 STEPS TO CYBER SECURITY

The '10 Steps to Cyber Security' advice originates from CESG, which is the Information Security arm of GCHQ, and the National Technical Authority for Information Assurance within the UK.

The measures detailed in the cyber security advice sheets collectively represent a good foundation for effective information risk management. The degree of implementation of these steps will vary between organisations depending on their risks to the individual business. However, GCHQ's recommendation is that boards should require their CIO and CISO to be able to articulate why a particular measure is not applicable.

The 10 areas are:

Home and mobile working:

- Develop a mobile working policy and train staff to adhere to it.
- Apply the secure baseline build to all devices.
- Protect data both in transit and at rest.

User education and awareness:

- Produce user security policies covering acceptable and secure use of the organisation's systems.
- Establish a staff training programme.
- Maintain user awareness of the cyber risks.

Incident management:

- Establish an incident response and disaster recovery capability.
- Produce and test IM plans.
- Provide specialist training to the IM team.
- Report criminal incidents to law enforcement agencies.

Managing user privileges:

- Establish account management processes and limit the number of privileged accounts.
- Limit user privileges and monitor user activity.
- Control access to activity and audit logs.

Removable media controls:

- Produce a policy to control all access to removable media.
- Limit media types and use.
- Scan all media for malware before importing onto corporate systems.

Monitoring:

- Establish a monitoring strategy and produce supporting policies.
- Continuously monitor all ICT systems and networks.
- Analyse logs for unusual activity that could indicate an attack.

Secure configuration:

- Apply security patches and ensure that the security configuration of all ICT systems is maintained.
- Create a system inventory and define a baseline build for all ICT devices.

Malware protection:

- Produce relevant policy and establish anti-malware defences that are applicable and relevant to all business areas.
- Scan for malware across the organisation.

Network security:

- Protect networks against external attack.
- Manage the network perimeter.
- Filter out unauthorised access and malicious content.
- Monitor and test security controls.

Information risk management regime:

- Establish an effective governance structure and determine risk appetite – just as for any other risk.
- Produce supporting information risk management policies.

There are three documents currently available:

- *Cyber risk management: a board-level responsibility.*
- *10 Steps to Cyber Security: executive companion.*
- *10 Steps to Cyber Security: advice sheets.*

The HMG Cyber Essentials scheme:

https://www.gov.uk/government/publications/cyber-essentials-scheme-overview [27 June 2014].

The 10 Steps to Cyber Security:

https://www.gov.uk/government/publications/cyber-risk-management-a-board-level-responsibility [27 June 2014].

APPENDIX H
REFERENCES AND FURTHER READING

I have attempted to include a number of useful references and items for further reading in this section. Where articles and documents are downloadable, I have provided the appropriate URL, but the reader should be aware that some organisations make regular changes to their websites and these links cannot be guaranteed. Where appropriate, I have provided a brief synopsis of the material listed.

The reference material falls into the following areas:

- primary UK legislation;
- good Practice Guidelines;
- the CESG Certified Professional Scheme;
- other UK Government publications;
- risk management methodologies;
- news articles, etc;
- other reference material;
- UK and international standards.

PRIMARY UK LEGISLATION

Data Protection Act 1998. Her Majesty's Stationery Office. Available from: http://www.legislation.gov.uk/ukpga/1998/29/contents [15 June 2014].

The Computer Misuse Act 1990. Her Majesty's Stationery Office. Available from: http://www.legislation.gov.uk/ukpga/1990/18/contents [15 June 2014].

The Police and Criminal Evidence Act 1984. Her Majesty's Stationery Office. Available from: http://www.legislation.gov.uk/ukpga/1984/60/contents [15 June 2014].

The Official Secrets Act 1989. Her Majesty's Stationery Office. Available from: http://www.legislation.gov.uk/ukpga/1989/6/contents [15 June 2014].

The Freedom of Information Act 2000. Her Majesty's Stationery Office. Available from: http://www.legislation.gov.uk/ukpga/2000/36/contents [15 June 2014].

The Regulation of Investigatory Powers Act 2000. Her Majesty's Stationery Office. Available from: http://www.legislation.gov.uk/ukpga/2000/23/contents [15 June 2014].

The Copyright, Designs and Patents Act 1988. Her Majesty's Stationery Office. Available from: http://www.legislation.gov.uk/ukpga/1988/48/contents [15 June 2014].

Control Of Major Accident Hazards Regulations 1999. Health and Safety Executive. Available from: http://www.legislation.gov.uk/uksi/1999/743/contents/made [15 June 2014].

Civil Contingencies Act 2004. Her Majesty's Stationery Office. Available from: http://www.legislation.gov.uk/ukpga/2004/36/contents [15 June 2014].

GOOD PRACTICE GUIDELINES

Good Practice Guidelines 2013. The Business Continuity Institute. Available from: https://shop.thebci.org/shop/shop.php?sid=144 [15 June 2014].

Synopsis: This document is considered by many to be the definitive work on BCM. It has undergone several iterations during its lifetime, and has been consistent in its approach, whilst keeping in step with developments and standards. The document is free to Business Continuity Institute members.

OTHER REFERENCE MATERIAL

The Traffic Light Protocol (TLP). Department of Homeland Security. Available from: http://www.us-cert.gov/tlp [15 June 2014].

Synopsis: The TLP is used internationally to represent the sensitivity of information and under what circumstances it may be shared with other parties. It is not designed to replace an information classification scheme, but is used especially when sharing security-related information with partners. The description of the TLP also appears in ISO/IEC 27010:2012.

The Capability Maturity Model. Carnegie Mellon University.

Synopsis: The Capability Maturity Model (CMM) was originally developed as a tool for assessing the performance of organisations developing software for the US Department of Defense. It can be adapted for many uses, and many organisations have adopted it for such areas as BCM and information risk management.

Critical Security Controls Version 5.0. The Council on CyberSecurity. Available from: http://www.cpni.gov.uk/documents/publications/2014/2014–04–11–critical–security–controls.pdf?epslanguage=en–gb [15 June 2014].

Synopsis: Developed mainly by the US military community, the list of critical security controls was compiled in order to reduce the data losses experienced by the American defence industrial base. Their use is free under creative commons, and many organisations worldwide have now adopted them as good practice recommendations, including the CPNI in the UK.

The IISP Skills Framework. The Institute of Information Security Professionals. Available from: https://www.iisp.org/imis15/iisp/About_Us/Our_Skills_Framework/iisp/About_Us/Our_Skills_Framework.aspx?hkey=6a996e64-4c90-4892-bb7e-b3d6e5dff3d5 [15 June 2014].

Synopsis: The IISP Skills Framework was developed by the Institute as a means of assessing potential members for their skills and experience in the information security industry. The framework consists of four levels of skill – awareness, basic application, skilful application and expert – and assesses skills in information security management, information risk management, implementing secure systems, IA methodologies and testing, operational security management, IM, audit, assurance and review, BCM, information systems research and teamwork and leadership. The framework is used for assessment in the CCP scheme.

A Structured Approach to Enterprise Risk Management (ERM) and the Requirements of ISO 31000. Airmic. Available from: http://www.airmic.com/guide/structured-approach-Enterprise-Risk-Management-ERM-requirements-ISO-31000 [15 June 2014].

Synopsis: Following the publication of the ISO 31000 Risk Management Principles and Guidelines, in 2009, a new document 'A Structured Approach to Enterprise Risk Management (ERM) and the Requirements of ISO 31000' has been produced by IRM, AIRMIC and Alarm that provides up-to-date guidance on the implementation of ERM in the context of the new ISO standard.

The Standard for Information Assurance for Small and Medium Sized Enterprises (IASME) Issue 2.3-2013. Available from: https://www.iasme.co.uk/images/docs/IASME Standard 2.3.pdf [2 July 2014].

Synopsis: Much of the documentation available refers mainly to larger organisations and Government. This standard is aimed specifically at SMEs, and claims conformance with ISO/IEC 27001 (the 2005 version); PAS 555; CESG's '10 Steps to Cyber Security'; and CPNI/SANS 20 'Critical Controls for Cyber Defence'.

Whilst not going into great detail on the risk assessment and risk treatment topics, it does provide useful high-level pointers to what SMEs should do to achieve one of six levels of maturity (0 to 5).

CESG CERTIFIED PROFESSIONAL SCHEME

Several of these documents are described in greater detail in Chapter 11.

CESG Certified Professional Scheme. CESG. Available from: http://www.cesg.gov.uk/awarenesstraining/certified-professionals/Pages/index.aspx [15 June 2014].

CESG Certification for IA Professionals. Issue No: 4.0 (March 2014). CESG. Available from: http://www.cesg.gov.uk/publications/Documents/cesg_certification_for_ia_professionals.pdf [15 June 2014].

Synopsis: CESG is the information security arm of GCHQ, and runs the CCP scheme, which is 'a certification which is awarded to those who demonstrate their sustained ability to apply their skills, knowledge and expertise in real-world situations'. It makes use of the IISP Skills Framework for the accreditation process. BCS, the Chartered Institute for IT, is one of the three organisations approved by CESG to carry out certification.

HMG IA Standard Numbers 1 & 2 – Information Risk Management Issue No: 4.0 (April 2012). Although unclassified, this document is not available online and must be requested directly from CESG.

Synopsis: This document is aimed at practitioners in IA and information risk management who work with ICT systems or services that handle, store or process government information. An important part of the Security Policy Framework, it contains 20 risk management requirements (RMRs), with which government departments or agencies must comply. Anyone wishing to be accredited as a CCP would be expected to be very familiar with this standard.

HMG IA Standard Numbers 1 & 2 – Supplement: Technical Risk Assessment Issue No. 1.0 (April 2012). Also unclassified, this document is not available online and must be requested directly from CESG.

Synopsis: This document is designed to be read in conjunction with *HMG IA Standard Numbers 1 & 2 – Information Risk Management*, and describes the concepts used in the technical risk assessment methodology and the risk assessment methodology itself, which consists of six stages: the concepts used in the risk treatment methodology; the risk treatment methodology itself; the Baseline Control Set; Business Impact Level tables; Modelling technique; and example forms.

Good Practice Guide 47 – Information Risk Management Issue No. 1.0 (April 2012). Also unclassified, this document is not available online and must be requested directly from CESG.

Synopsis: The GPG covers departmental IA policies, standards, guidance and procedures; information risk management shared services; accreditation; mandatory and specialist security roles, responsibilities and functions. It also provides an example Risk Management Accreditation Document Set (RMADS) and examples of information risk appetite statements.

OTHER UK GOVERNMENT PUBLICATIONS

Several of these documents are described in greater detail in Chapter 11.

'HMG Security Policy Framework Version 11.0 (October 2013)'. Government Digital Service. Available from: https://www.gov.uk/government/publications/security-policy-framework [15 June 2014].

Synopsis: This is the overarching framework for many other government documents and standards. It describes the security controls that must be applied to all government assets, and consists of four key policy areas: governance and security approaches;

security of information; personnel security; and physical security and counter-terrorism. Within these policy areas are 20 mandatory requirements (MRs).

'Government Security Classifications (April 2014)'. Government Digital Service. Available from: https://www.gov.uk/government/publications/government-security-classifications [15 June 2014].

Synopsis: Until quite recently, the government classified information into five categories: Unclassified, Restricted, Confidential, Secret and Top Secret. The updated classification scheme simplifies the scheme and reduces the number of categories to three: Official, Secret and Top Secret. This is reflected in the updated version of the Security Policy Framework.

'HM Treasury, Orange Book: Management of Risk – Principles and Concepts, October 2004'. Government Digital Service. Available from: https://www.gov.uk/government/publications/green-book-supplementary-guidance-risk [15 June 2014].

Synopsis: Not as prescriptive as the other government documents, the Orange Book is an excellent guide to risk management from HM Treasury. Now over 10 years old, it still has considerable value and uses plain language to describe the risk management process.

The HMG Cyber Essentials scheme. Available from: https://www.gov.uk/government/publications/cyber-essentials-scheme-overview [27 June 2014].

'The 10 Steps to Cyber Security'. Available from: https://www.gov.uk/government/publications/cyber-risk-management-a-board-level-responsibility [27 June 2014].

RISK MANAGEMENT METHODOLOGIES

These methodologies are described in greater detail in Appendix B.

CORAS Risk Assessment Platform. SourceForge. Available from: http://coras.sourceforge.net/index.html [15 June 2014].

CRAMM (CCTA Risk Analysis and Management Method). Siemens Insight Consulting. Available from: Siemens Insight Consulting.

FAIR (Factor Analysis of Information Risk). Risk Management Insight. Available from: http://www.riskmanagementinsight.com/media/docs/FAIR_introduction.pdf [15 June 2014].

IRAM (Information Risk Analysis Method), The Information Security Forum. Available from: https://www.securityforum.org/tools/isf-risk-manager/ [15 June 2014].

The OCTAVE Method (Operationally Critical Threat, Asset and Vulnerability Evaluation). Carnegie Mellon University. Available from: http://www.cert.org/resilience/products-services/octave/octave-method.cfm [15 June 2014].

The OCTAVE-S Method – designed for use by smaller organisations. Carnegie Mellon University. Available from: http://www.cert.org/resilience/products-services/octave/octave-s-method.cfm [15 June 2014].

The OCTAVE Allegro Method, a streamlined approach for information security assessment and assurance. Carnegie Mellon University. Available from: http://www.cert.org/resilience/products-services/octave/octave-allegro-method.cfm [15 June 2014].

SABSA (Sherwood Applied Business Security Architecture). The SABSA Institute. Available from: http://www.sabsa.org/white_paper [15 June 2014] (Requires form submission).

NEWS ARTICLES ETC.

The BP Deepwater Horizon oil disaster. Available from: http://www.bbc.co.uk/news/special_reports/oil_disaster/

Gerald Ratner's 1991 gaffe. Available from: http://www.inspiringinterns.com/blog/2012/10/'doing-a-ratner'-6-business-publicity-disasters/

Donald Rumsfeld on things we don't now. Available from: http://www.brainyquote.com/quotes/quotes/d/donaldrums148142.html

The eBay data breach. Available from: http://www.bbc.co.uk/news/technology-27539799

UK AND INTERNATIONAL STANDARDS

The first part of this section lists and briefly describes some of the ISO/IEC 27000 series standards, especially those that are part of the so-called ISMS Family of Standards and including those in the 2703x range, which specify control-specific requirements.

- Vocabulary standards:
  - ISO/IEC 27000:2014 – Information technology – Security techniques – Information security management systems – Overview and vocabulary.

    Synopsis: This standard includes three main sections. First, there are the Terms and Definitions. It then describes the purpose and approach to establishing an Information Security Management System (ISMS). Finally, it itemises and describes the 27000 family of standards that are relevant to an ISMS.
- Requirement standards:
  - ISO/IEC 27001:2013 – Information technology – Security techniques – Information security management systems – Requirements.

    Synopsis: This standard is recognised as the main document for the establishment, implementation, operation, monitoring, review, maintenance and improvement of an ISMS. It is against this standard that organisations can be audited and certified. The annex to the document lists 114 separate controls in 14 categories, including the control objectives. This list is greatly enhanced in ISO/IEC 27002, which expands the detail of each control by providing implementation guidance (see Guideline standards).

- ISO/IEC 27006:2011 – Information technology – Security techniques – Requirements for bodies providing audit and certification of information security management systems.

  Synopsis: Aimed those bodies who provide certification, this standard guides auditors through the process of conducting an ISMS audit against ISO/IEC 27001. In particular, it provides guidance on the complexity of audit scope depending on the size of the organisation concerned, areas of competence required by auditors in this area and the likely time it will take to undertake an audit. For all 114 controls, it details whether they are organisational or technical controls, whether they can be verified through system testing and whether visual inspection of documentation is required, and provides further guidance on areas where such information is likely to be found.

  The standard makes several references to ISO/IEC 17021:2011 – Conformity assessment – Requirements for bodies providing audit and certification of management systems.

- Guideline standards:

  - ISO/IEC 27002:2013 – Information technology – Security techniques – Code of Practice for Information Security Management.

    Synopsis: This standard contains the recommended best practice controls for treatment of risks in an ISMS. Each of the 114 controls listed in ISO/IEC 27001 is repeated, together with implementation guidance.

  - ISO/IEC 27003:2010 – Information technology – Security techniques – Information security management system implementation guidance.

    Synopsis: As the title suggests, this standard provides guidance on the establishment, implementation, operation, monitoring, review, maintenance and improvement of an ISMS. It includes a useful section on the preparation of business cases, and continues with the inputs required, outputs delivered and guidance on the various stages of the ISMS. It contains a detailed checklist, together with information regarding roles and responsibilities, internal audit, policy structure and monitoring and measuring.

  - ISO/IEC 27004:2009 – Security techniques – Information security management – Measurement.

    Synopsis: Based on the PDCA model, this standard provides suggestions as to how the effectiveness of some information risk controls can be measured, and provides a number of templates for achieving this.

  - ISO/IEC 27005:2011 – Information security risk management (based on and incorporating ISO/IEC 13335 MICTS Part 2).

    Synopsis: As the standard for information security risk management, ISO/IEC 27005 is an essential part of the ISO/IEC 27000 series, and encourages organisations to follow the well-established process to ensure that their information security management system reflects and manages the risks to the organisation's information.

  - ISO/IEC 27007:2011 – Information technology – Security techniques – Guidelines for information security management systems auditing.

    Synopsis: Whilst ISO/IEC 27006 is aimed at certification bodies, this standard is aimed more at the internal audit community, and provides advice and guidance on the audit criteria for each area, any relevant standards that apply, the evidence they should find and practical guidance on how to approach the audit. It makes a number of references to ISO 19011:2011 – Guidelines for auditing management systems.

- ISO/IEC TR 27008: – Information Technology – Security techniques – Guidelines for auditors on information security controls.

    Synopsis: Whereas the previous standard deals with the process for auditing an ISMS, this technical report examines the audit approach to verifying individual controls. It provides examples of the requirement of a number of controls, some additional technical explanations of the reason for the controls' use, the security implementation standard expected together with any additional technical supporting information, the practice guidance, evidence assumed and the method to be adopted. It also provides guidance on initial information gathering that falls outside the IT environment.

- ISO/IEC 27013 – Information technology– Security techniques – Guidance on the integrated implementation of ISO/IEC 27001 and ISO/IEC 20000-1.

    Synopsis: This standard deals with the joint implementation of both ISO/IEC 27001 and ISO/IEC 20000-1:2011 – (Information technology – Service management – Part 1: Service management system requirements), which may already have been implemented by an organisation. The standard allows for three options: to implement ISO/IEC 27001 when ISO/IEC 20000-1 has already been implemented; to implement both ISO/IEC 27001 and ISO/IEC 20000-1 together; to align both the ISO/IEC 27001 and ISO/IEC 20000-1 implementations.

- ISO/IEC 27014 – Information technology – Security techniques – Governance of information security.

    Synopsis: This standard deals with how the senior management of an organisation can manage the relationship between organisation governance, governance of information technology and governance of information security.

- ISO/IEC TR 27016 – Information technology – Security techniques – Information security management – Organisational economics.

    Synopsis: This is a technical report as opposed to a standard, and provides guidance on how organisations can use the impact assessment information to create business cases and then better compare the costs of protection with the potential costs of an incident.

- Sector-specific guideline standards:

    - ISO/IEC 27010:2012 – Information technology – Security techniques – Information security management for inter-sector and inter-organisational communications.

        Synopsis: ISO/IEC deals extremely well with the requirements for an ISMS within organisations, but does not specifically address the concept of information shared between organisations, either on a one-to-one or a many-to-many basis, especially in situations where both are cognisant of the sensitivity of the information being shared. This standard addresses this subject area, discusses the concept of anonymising information in order to protect its source and deals with the concept of trust in information sharing communities. Additionally, it is the first ISO standard to describe the use of the TLP, which is discussed in Chapter 2 of this book.

- ISO/IEC 27011:2008 – Information technology – Security techniques – Information security management guidelines for telecommunications organisations based on ISO/IEC 27002.

  Synopsis: The first sector-specific guideline standard, this is a direct copy-and-paste of the International Telecommunications Union (ITU) Standard X.1051 of 2008. It includes sections on the organisation of information security; asset management; human resources security; communications and operations management; access control; information systems acquisition; development and maintenance; information security IM; BCM; and compliance. The document finishes by describing some additional controls that are relevant to the telecommunications sector, together with some additional implementation guidance.

- ISO/IEC 27015 – Information technology. Security techniques. Information security management guidelines for financial services.

  Synopsis: Another sector-specific guideline standard currently available, ISO/IEC 27015 I aimed at initiation, implementation, maintenance and improvement of an ISMS within financial organisations.

- Control-specific guideline standards:

- ISO/IEC 27031:2011 – Information technology – Security techniques – Guidelines for information and communication technology readiness for business continuity.

  Synopsis: This standard is one of the first to examine the world of DR, and addresses the concept of ICT Readiness for Business Continuity (IRBC). It includes references to five other ISO/IEC standards.

- ISO/IEC 27032:2012 – Information technology – Security techniques – Guidelines for cybersecurity.

  Synopsis: This standard relates specifically to cybersecurity, which it defines as a 'complex environment resulting from the interaction of people, software and services on the Internet by means of technology devices and networks connected to it, which do not exist in any physical form'.

  It would be easy to assume that this dealt solely with technology issues, but it deals with all types of operational controls – people/procedural, physical/environmental and technical/logical.

- ISO/IEC 27033 – Information technology – Security techniques – Network security.

  Synopsis: This group of five standards relate to network security and date from 2009 to 2014. The first provides an overview and concepts; the second provides guidelines for the design and implementation of network security; the third addresses reference networking scenarios (threats, design techniques and control issues); the fourth provides guidance on securing communications between networks using security gateways; and the final one examines securing communications across networks using VPNs.

- ISO/IEC 27034:2011 – Information technology – Security techniques – Application security – Part 1: Overview and concepts.

  Synopsis: The title of this standard indicates that there should be several parts, but at the moment, this is the only one available. It is intended to assist organisations in the integration of security into the processes used for managing their applications, and introduces definitions, concepts, principles and processes, but stops short of providing guidelines for secure software application development.

- ISO/IEC 27035:2011 – Information technology – Security techniques – Information security incident management.

  Synopsis: The standard is aimed at helping organisations to deal with information security incidents by introducing a structured approach, including planning and preparation, detection and reporting, assessment and decision-making, response and learning lessons. It provides some examples of information security incidents and their causes; lists a number of information security incident classification types; provides templates for recording and reporting incidents; and addresses the legal and regulatory aspects of information security IM.

- ISO/IEC 27036 – Information technology – Security techniques – Information security for supplier relationships.

  Synopsis: This standard comes in three parts: overview and concepts; common requirements (currently still in draft form); and guidelines for information and communication technology supply chain security.

- ISO/IEC 27037 – Information technology – Security techniques – Guidelines for identification, collection, acquisition and preservation of digital evidence.

  Synopsis: Although some organisations do not wish the fact that they have suffered an information security incident, many are now ensuring that they are able to collect evidence of such an incident in a manner that will enable a successful prosecution. This standard provides guidelines that will enable organisations to undertake this in a manner that is considered forensically acceptable.

- ISO/IEC 27038 – Information technology – Security techniques – Specification for digital redaction.

  Synopsis: Occasionally, organisations are required through legal and regulatory or other routes to release documents for public consumption; for example, under the Freedom of Information Act (FoIA). If these documents contain some sensitive information, but are otherwise able to be made public, then it is possible to redact the sensitive information.

  This standard provides guidelines for the principles and processes associated with redaction, together with the characteristics of software redaction tools and the requirements for redaction testing.

- ISO 22301:2012 – Societal security – Business continuity management systems – Requirements.

  Synopsis: This standard replaced BS 25999-2 in 2012, and is now regarded worldwide as the definitive business continuity standard. In the 12 months since its publication, many organisations that were previously accredited to BS 25999-2 have been successfully re-accredited to ISO 22301.

- Other relevant Standards:

- ISO/IEC 15504-2:2003 – Software engineering – Process assessment – Part 2: Performing an assessment.

  Synopsis: Whilst ISO/IEC 15504-2 is aimed primarily at process assessment in software engineering; the principles apply equally to information risk management. The capability levels described are very similar to those in the Capability Maturity Model from the CMMI Institute, and also to those used in COBIT 5.

- ISO/IEC Guide 73:2009 – Risk management – Vocabulary – Guidelines for use in standards.

Synopsis: ISO Guide 73:2009 provides the definitions of generic terms related to risk management. It aims to encourage a mutual and consistent understanding of, and a coherent approach to, the description of activities relating to the management of risk, and the use of uniform risk management terminology in processes and frameworks dealing with the management of risk.

- ISO 31000:2009 Risk management – Principles and guidelines.

Synopsis: ISO 31000 is the international standard for risk management. By providing comprehensive principles and guidelines, this standard helps organisations with their risk analysis and risk assessments. BS ISO 31000 applies to most business activities including planning, management operations and communication processes. Whilst all organisations manage risk to some extent, this international standard's best–practice recommendations were developed to improve management techniques and ensure safety and security in the workplace at all times.

- IEC 31010:2009 – Risk management – Risk assessment techniques.

Synopsis: Whilst not aimed specifically at information risk management, this standard goes into the generic risk management process in considerable detail. Much of the document is made up of the detailed techniques for undertaking the whole risk management programme, and each area covered is itemised and described in six different categories: overview; use; inputs; process; outputs; and strengths and weaknesses.

- BS 7799-3:2006 – Information security management systems – Guidelines for information security risk management.

Synopsis: This standard is the one upon which this book was based, and follows the structure of context establishment, risk identification, risk analysis, risk evaluation and risk treatment, together with communication and consultation and monitoring and review.

- BS 31100:2011 – Risk management – Code of practice and guidance for the implementation of BS ISO 31000.

Synopsis: BS 31100:2011 outlines a risk management process that can be used and interpreted so that each group within an organisation works in a manner that increases consistency and communication across the business.

- PAS 77:2006 – IT Service Continuity Management – Code of Practice.

Synopsis: This publicly available specification deals with DR in the IT environment. It defines service continuity management; describes the process for defining a service continuity strategy; covers risks and impacts within the organisation, and conducting business criticality and risk assessments; describes the key components of a service continuity plan and the requirement to rehearse this; and describes a number of solutions architecture and design considerations, including the purchase of continuity services. The annexes include sections on virtualisation, types of site models, high-availability systems and types of resilience.

- PAS 555:2013 – Cyber security risk – Governance and management. specification.

  Synopsis: Threats to an organisation's cyber security present a critical challenge in terms of scale, complexity and impact – with business assets such as corporate and customer data, IP, and brand and reputation at risk. It is crucial that an organisation understands and manages its exposure to cyber security threats.

- The Risk Management Standard. Available from: http://www.ferma.eu/risk-management/standards/risk-management-standard/ [16 June 2014].

  Synopsis: The Risk Management Standard was originally published by the Institute of Risk Management (IRM), The Association of Insurance and Risk Managers (AIRMIC) and Alarm (The Public Risk Management Association) in 2002. It has subsequently been adopted by the Federation of European Risk Management Associates (FERMA).

- Guide for Conducting Risk Assessments – NIST Special Publication 800-30 Revision 1 (September 2012). Available from: http://csrc.nist.gov/publications/nistpubs/800-30-rev1/sp800_30_r1.pdf [16 June 2014].

  Synopsis: This NIST standard deals with the fundamentals of risk management: the risk management process; risk assessment; key risk concepts and the application of risk assessments. It then examines the risk management process in greater detail: preparing for the risk assessment; conducting the risk assessment; communicating and sharing risk assessment information; and maintaining the risk assessment. In its appendices, the standard includes references; a glossary of terms; acronyms; threat sources; threat events; vulnerabilities and predisposing conditions; likelihood of occurrence; impact; risk determination, informing risk response; risk assessment reports; and a summary of tasks.

- Security and Privacy Controls for Federal Information Systems and Organisations – NIST Special Publication 800-53 Revision 4 (April 2013). Available from: http://nvlpubs.nist.gov/nistpubs/SpecialPublications/NIST. SP.800-53r4.pdf [16 June 2014].

  Synopsis: This NIST standard covers the fundamentals of security and privacy controls: assessments within the system development lifecycle; the strategy for conducting security control assessments; building an effective assurance case; and assessment procedures. It continues by describing the process: preparing for security control assessments; developing security assessment plans; conducting security control assessments; and analysing security assessment report results. In its appendixes, the standard includes references; a glossary of terms; acronyms; assessment method descriptions; penetration testing; an assessment procedure catalogue; security assessment reports; and assessment cases.

All British and ISO Standards may be purchased through British and ISO Standards can be obtained in PDF or hard copy formats from the BSI online shop, http://www.bsigroup. com/Shop, or by contacting BSI Customer Services for hardcopies only: Tel: +44 (0) 20 8996 9001, email: mailto:cservices@bsigroup.com.

It is worth pointing out that by joining BSI, members can enjoy a 50% discount on many BS products, and 10% discount on ISO Standards. Visit http://shop.bsigroup.com/ Navigate-by/Membership/ for more details.

INDEX